A SELF-DEVELOPMENT PROGRAMME

Effectivecommunication

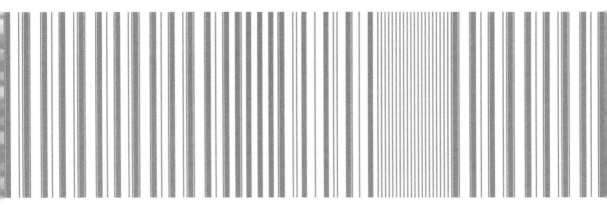

Acknowledgments

The following have contributed to the preparation of
this book or to the development of the approaches
taken in it:
Sheila & David Roebuck
Dr Paul Dobson; City University Business School
Stephen P. Robbins

A SELF-DEVELOPMENT PROGRAMME

Effectivecommunication

THE ESSENTIAL GUIDE TO THINKING AND WORKING SMARTER

Chris Roebuck

MARSHALL PUBLISHING • LONDON

Dedicated by the author to Sheila and David Roebuck

A Marshall Edition
Conceived, edited and designed by
Marshall Editions Ltd
The Orangery
161 New Bond Street
London W1Y 9PA

First published in the UK in 1998 by Marshall Publishing Ltd

Copyright © 1998
Marshall Editions
Developments Ltd

ISBN 1-84028-136-7

Series Consultant Editor
Chris Roebuck
Project Editor
Jo Wells at Axis Design
Designer
Martin Laurie at Axis Design
Art Director
Sean Keogh
Managing Art Editor
Patrick Carpenter
Managing Editor
Clare Currie
Editorial Assistant
Sophie Sandy
Editorial Coordinator
Becca Clunes
Production
Nikki Ingram
Cover Design
Poppy Jenkins

Originated in Italy by Articolor
Printed and bound in France by SIRC

Video Arts quotes extracted from training films:
p37 & 62: "The Business Letter Business"
pp44 & 55: "Straight Talking"
p67: "Report Writing"

Contents

1

**Achieving objectives
Inform people
Inform yourself
Develop skills**

Is effective communication important?

Will better communication benefit me?

How can I improve my skills?

Why Is Effective Communication Important?

The ability to communicate effectively is perhaps the most critical skill for anyone at work, indeed for life in general. Without communication nothing can be achieved. It is communication that holds our society together; without it we are just individuals relying on our own experiences to help us through life. The ability to communicate – to pass on ideas, experiences and feelings – has allowed the human race to develop.

Imagine the impact on your family and all the problems that it would cause if suddenly you were unable to communicate with each other. Phone messages would not get passed on, chores would not get done and money would be wasted as you and your partner duplicated the weekly shop.

An organization is just a group of people, and if the members don't communicate effectively, the same problems arise that would occur if a family did not communicate.

Poor communication leads to poor performance, yet it is common in the workplace. Happily, communication skills can be improved and the more effective the communication, the better the overall performance and the greater the level of achievement.

Team Leader
Planning • Organizing • Controlling • Motivating • Developing

Downward Communication
Flow of Plans • Instructions • Expectations

Feedback
Upward flow of Communication • Results • Expectations • Views and Ideas

Individual or Team
Performance

The same applies to individuals. The more effective you are at communicating, the more likely you are to be able to achieve what you want. Communication links the different stages when you do anything – from playing a game of football to chairing a meeting. In order to achieve your objectives there needs to be a flow of information in both directions.

Effective communication allows you to use all the other skills that you have to the full. The ability to motivate, delegate, organize, solve problems and obtain information, all rely on your ability to communicate with others. Unless you can communicate well you will find it very difficult to be effective at work, or even in your personal life.

Over 80 percent of our waking life is spent either sending or receiving information. To help you understand how important communication really is at work write a list of things you do at work that entail some communication. For example, taking and passing on a telephone message, writing a letter and contributing to a meeting. You can stop if you go over 25! Can you think of anything you do at work that does not include some communication?

Communication is a two-way process. As well as getting your own message across, it is also important to listen to and understand what others have to say – a technique known as "active listening". This will ensure that you can give other people what they want and that you get the information that you need.

Allowing other people to communicate effectively with you is just as important as ensuring that you can communicate effectively with them. For example, if your boss never bothered to listen to you, you would probably become very demotivated and things may start going wrong as a result. If your boss did not listen, then your problems (perhaps a lack of resources, late deliveries from suppliers, difficulties with other departments, or simply stress) would remain unknown and as a result would not be dealt with. Without asking how things are going and listening to the reply he or she will not even know whether you have accomplished the tasks that have been set. It is important to realize the potential effects that a lack of communication could have on your performance and that of the organization.

You already know from experience that poor communication can cause problems. How often have you been given unclear instructions by your boss? Have you ever misunderstood what colleagues are trying to say? How often have you asked somebody to do something in a way that you believed was quite clear and then discovered that they misunderstood you? How many times in the last week has there been some form of communication problem at work? What consequences resulted?

Will Improving My Skills Bring Benefits?

Effective communication can transform how well people work. Imagine an organization where everyone is kept informed, knows exactly what to do and has all the information necessary.

Think of a workplace where your ideas and suggestions are welcomed, other people offer you their help and knowledge and there is never any confusion, rumours, or worry about saying what you think about the way things are done.

THINK OF A GOOD COMMUNICATOR

Think of examples of bad communication that have happened in your life – note five incidents of bad communication that you have experienced. Try to identify what went wrong and the consequences.

Also, think about individuals you have known who were good communicators – maybe a boss or a teacher. Give examples of their effective communication, the benefits that this brought to you, and how it helped you to work better.

Writing down experiences of both good and bad communication, what made them good or bad and the benefits or consequences, will help you to focus on how well you communicate. Think about the experiences you have written down and ask yourself "Do I do it like this?"

Sharing knowledge is critical to success. If, rather than keeping quiet, people shared their knowledge with others, the experienced helped the inexperienced and problems were solved using everyone's knowledge, this would dramatically speed up the skills development of less experienced people, allow more delegation and get problems solved quickly.

Just think of the energy, freedom and enthusiasm that such an organization would encourage. Now think what effect it would have on the performance of the organization that you work in if everyone within it felt motivated and worked in this environment – it would be a great place to work. This is what effective communication can achieve. In the real world some companies have realized this and have invested a great deal of time, effort and money on improving their communication.

Bad communication, in any form, carries the risk of wasting time and resources – the wrong thing being done – or causing conflict between people. Both reduce the team's ability to get the job done, and can cause lasting harm if relationships break down. Evidence suggests that bad communication is probably the cause of most of the problems that people encounter at work.

THE COSTS OF BAD COMMUNICATION

People aren't clear on what they should do which leads to wasted time and wasted resources

People misunderstand what is being said which leads to bad working relationships

People don't communicate ideas and knowledge which leads to slow skills development and problems take a long time to solve

People don't know why they are doing things

Staff morale drops which leads to high staff turnover

The organization is unresponsive and inflexible which leads to a bad image with customers and clients and a loss of business

BENEFITS OF EFFECTIVE COMMUNICATION

Everyone knows what they should be doing

Everyone understands why they are doing what they do and how this fits in with the organization's goals

The resources are in the right place at the right time

You have all the relevant information to do the job

Any idea that can improve performance will be welcomed and used

People learn and develop skills faster

Problems are solved quickly using all the knowledge within the organization

The organization is flexible and can respond quickly

How Can I Improve My Skills?

Even though you may already be a good communicator, everyone can always be better. Perhaps you assume that you communicate well, but it is likely that you rarely, if ever, assess how well you actually perform. This is your opportunity to see how well you are doing at the moment and to improve your skills where required.

Improving how you communicate with others is much easier than you think. In many ways you already have a lot of experience of communicating. You have been involved in social communication since childhood. This will have helped you understand some of the basics, but for effective business communication these existing skills need to be fine tuned in order to get the message across in the best way and so that you can achieve what you want to.

In chapter two you will be able to assess how you are doing in all the major areas of communication that you encounter at work. Then chapters three and four will help you to understand how to communicate effectively in these areas, help you to put together a plan to develop your skills, and show you how to improve the communication skills of all of the members of your team.

You can build up your skills across the major areas of communication – from writing reports to using the telephone. Use the self-assessments, ideas and checklists, in order to regularly assess how your skills have developed and to help you in the future. The way you will improve your skills is by using simple formats that you can transfer effectively to work. In addition you will also be able to understand the principles behind how the communication process works. This will allow you to be effective in

Build On Your Experience   **Regularly Assess Your Skills**

situations that may not be covered by this book.

The most effective way of improving is to assess your skills, which are based on previous experiences you have had, identify and improve on your areas of weakness and capitalize on your strengths. This will allow you to target the time and effort that you put into developing your skills, concentrating on where it is really needed – and where it will bring the most benefit. This process will also accustom you to organizing your own self-development so that in the future you can take control of your own development if required. You may assume that your organization will take care of your development, however many organizations do not do so, or at least not in the most effective way. You should always be aware of your own needs so that if the organization does not develop you fully you can plan your own improvement.

Being a good communicator is a joy, not a chore. Getting your ideas across, helping other people and achieving your ambitions all come with effective communication. Think of a time when you have helped someone overcome a problem by giving them advice, and the satisfaction that you obtained when the problem was solved – communication made that possible.

That new team member who you helped to become an expert in some area, the time you helped your boss to appreciate the benefits of delegating more responsibility to the team, the first team meeting you successfully ran when your boss was away – all were made possible with effective communication. If you put the effort in to develop your skills the benefits will be substantial.

Capitalize On Your Strengths + Improve Your Weak Areas

= Communicate More Effectively

2

Self-assessment
Strengths
Weaknesses
Feedback

How well do I communicate verbally?

Am I a good listener?

How good is my written work?

Why Is Self-Assessment Important?

To improve your skills you need to know how good you are. A general self-assessment will enable you to identify your strengths and weaknesses. Then you can plan how to improve. Each assessment focuses on one area of communication.

Tick whichever of the suggested answers best describes what you do. The assessment process will only benefit you if you are honest. At the end of each section analyze your answers and hone your understanding of your own skills.

Face-to-face with another person

Most communication is carried out face-to-face with other individuals; asking for information, offering advice, your annual performance appraisal, or telling someone what you think of their performance, all tend to be done in a one-to-one situation. This is one of the most critical areas of communication to get right. With a little help most people can greatly improve the way they communicate one-to-one. Assess how you are doing at present.

Question	usually	sometimes	seldom
1 Do you find that people get the "wrong end of the stick" and misunderstand you?			
2 Do you find that when talking to others you lose the thread of what you are trying to say?			
3 Do people come back and ask for further clarification of what you have said?			
4 Are you ever sarcastic?			
5 Do you avoid using face-to-face communication?			
6 Do you try to phrase what you say and deliver it in a way that you think is appropriate to the person you are talking to?			

How Did You Score?

Questions 1–5		Questions 6–12	
Usually	1 point	Usually	3 points
Sometimes	2 points	Sometimes	2 points
Seldom	3 points	Seldom	1 point

More than 32
Your one-to-one communication skills seem to be good. There may be room for improvement in some areas.

26–32
You have some skills, but you could achieve considerable improvements.

Under 26
Your skills need substantial improvement in many areas.

	Question	usually	sometimes	seldom
7	Do you maintain eye contact when you speak to someone?			
8	Do you ever ask the person who you are talking to whether they have understood what you said?			
9	Do you try to find an appropriate time and place to talk?			
10	Do you ever tell people why you are asking them to do something?			
11	If what you need to tell someone is difficult, complicated or both, do you plan it first?			
12	Do you ask people for their views?			

Face-to-Face With A Group

Communicating face-to-face with a group of people can be an intimidating thing to do, whether it is a group of new customers, or the people that you work with all the time. In such a stressful situation it is easy to forget things and make mistakes. It is probably the most intimidating form of communication that you have to do, but it can be a valuable way of providing information to everyone or canvassing the opinion of a wide range of staff on one particular issue. It also means that everyone is getting the same information, which removes the potential for confusion.

As a team leader you need to be effective at communicating with a group – that's what your team is. With practice even the most nervous person will be able to happily address their team and other groups. Don't try to get out of it, practice makes perfect. If you follow the advice given in this book, you will be able to create a structure that you are familiar with and can rely on. When it becomes automatic you will have beaten your nerves and may even start to enjoy speaking to a group. Feedback is just as important when talking to a group as when you are talking one-to-one, so plan some time into your agenda to answer questions and to ask for opinions from your audience.

	Question	usually	sometimes	seldom
1	I am nervous about speaking to a group.			
2	If we have to hold a team meeting, I let the team know about the meeting well in advance.			
3	Some team members don't contribute to meetings.			
4	I plan in advance what I am going to say at any team meeting.			
5	In team meetings I do all the talking.			

How Did You Score?

Questions 1, 3, 5, 7, 8,10		Questions 2, 4, 6, 9	
Usually	1 point	Usually	3 points
Sometimes	2 points	Sometimes	2 points
Seldom	3 points	Seldom	1 point

More than 26
Your direct communication skills in a group seem to be good. But there may be room for improvement in some areas.

20-26
You have some skills, but you could achieve considerable improvements.

Under 20
Your skills need substantial improvement in many areas.

	Question	usually	sometimes	seldom
6	After I brief my team they never ask for more information or clarification.			
7	I let anyone speak as much as they like at meetings.			
8	I let people argue to clear the air.			
9	I always ask if there are issues people want to discuss other than mine.			
10	I always treat each group of people I speak to in the same way.			

Giving Feedback

If you want to manage other people effectively, it is essential that you give them feedback. The major complaint of most individuals about their boss is that they are rarely told how they are doing on a day-to-day basis. Most say "I'd rather know if I am doing badly – at least I'd know one way or the other".

If you don't give feedback, how can people know that things are going wrong, or (hopefully) well? Giving positive feedback (praise) is easy, it is the negative feedback that we all try to avoid giving. Don't fall into this trap. The team would rather know than not. How can they get better if you don't tell them? It is essential to deal with problems as soon as they arise with well-planned negative feedback, rather than allowing the problem to build up.

It is also essential in terms of motivation to let your team know when they are performing well. Give praise where it is due.

	Question	usually	sometimes	seldom
1	I focus my comments on specific job-related events.			
2	I keep my comments descriptive and subjective rather than using evaluations or figures.			
3	I prefer to save up comments so that they can be presented and discussed in detail at the person's annual performance review.			
4	I always ensure that my feedback is clearly understood.			
5	I supplement criticisms with suggestions on what the person can do to improve.			
6	My feedback focuses on the person's past performance and not on future potential.			

How Did You Score?

Questions 2, 3, 6, 9, 11		Questions 1, 4, 5, 7, 8, 10, 12	
Usually	1 point	Usually	3 points
Sometimes	2 points	Sometimes	2 points
Seldom	3 points	Seldom	1 point

More than 32
Your feedback skills seem to be good. But there may be room for improvement in some areas.

26–32
You have some skills, but you could achieve considerable improvements.

Under 26
Your skills need substantial improvement in many areas.

	Question	usually	sometimes	seldom
7	I always try to find something positive to say even if there are negatives.			
8	I always ask for the other person's views on my feedback.			
9	Rather than getting into a discussion, I always tell the individual concerned how I want them to behave in the future.			
10	I ask the other person for their views on their performance before I give them mine.			
11	I find it difficult to give negative feedback when I should.			
12	I give praise if someone has done well.			

Using The Telephone

The telephone is one of the mainstays of modern business communication. Everyone uses the telephone, but not everyone uses it well or at the appropriate times.

To get the maximum benefit from the telephone you need to make sure that you use it to both benefit yourself and to help those who call you. When you call you can help the person at the other end to do what you want by handling the call effectively yourself. The success or failure of the call depends just as much on the way you approach the other person as it does on them. When someone calls you they will have an objective and if you can help them to achieve this they will get a positive impression of both you and your organization. For example, if a customer rings to order some equipment, but is not sure what they need and you help them to decide, they will be pleased with the outcome of the call. A telephone conversation requires more concentration than a face-to-face meeting because you do not have any of the additional signals from body language to help you understand the message. No matter how inconvenient devote your full attention to the call for the few minutes that it lasts and make notes to ensure that you remember the key points of the conversation.

	Question	usually	sometimes	seldom
1	I let the telephone ring at least five times before answering.			
2	When I answer I give my name, department and ask how I can help.			
3	To save time I often read memos or letters whilst on the phone.			
4	When calling other people I always check that it is convenient for them to speak.			
5	I always try to keep the call short even if it means interrupting the caller.			

How Did You Score?

Questions 1, 3, 5, 7, 8		Questions 2, 4, 6, 9, 10	
Usually	1 point	Usually	3 points
Sometimes	2 points	Sometimes	2 points
Seldom	3 points	Seldom	1 point

More than 26
Your telephone skills seem to be good, but there may be room for improvement in some areas.

26–32
You have some skills, but you could achieve considerable improvements.

Under 26
Your skills need substantial improvement in many areas.

	Question	usually	sometimes	seldom
6	I ask for clarification if I don't understand what the caller has said.			
7	If the call is long or complex, I find that I sometimes lose track.			
8	I never bother to write down messages because I remember them.			
9	I update and check my voicemail or answerphone regularly.			
10	I always write down what I have to do straight after the call.			

Written Communication

Lots of people are nervous about committing themselves to paper. Anxiety about making mistakes with punctuation, spelling and grammar should not prevent you from using the right type of communication to best get the message across. In many cases this is written communication. It may take more time than a conversation, but putting your thoughts in writing can have the advantage of forcing you to really think about what you are saying before it reaches the other person.

You have probably said something and then thought "Hang on, that wasn't really what I meant to say", or "Oh dear that wasn't a very intelligent comment".

With written communication you have more chances to get it right – make sure that you use them.

It's a common misconception that a written message needs to be more complicated than if it were delivered face-to-face. This can lead to long-winded letters which only confuse. Stick to clear language, avoiding jargon that the other person will not understand. Keep it simple and logical and you are more likely to be successful.

Keeping a written record of complicated communications can be invaluable. How many times have you had to refer back to a message or information source?

	Question	usually	sometimes	seldom
1	I avoid writing things if I can.			
2	People come back and ask me to clarify what I have written.			
3	I plan what I am going to write before I start.			
4	I send off the first thing I write.			
5	My written communications are full of long and technical words.			

How Did You Score?

Questions 1, 2, 4, 5, 8		Questions 3, 6, 7, 9, 10	
Usually	1 point	Usually	3 points
Sometimes	2 points	Sometimes	2 points
Seldom	3 points	Seldom	1 point

More than 26
Your written skills seem to be good, but there may be room for improvement in some areas.

26–32
You have some skills, but you could achieve considerable improvements.

Under 26
Your skills need substantial improvement in many areas.

	Question	usually	sometimes	seldom
6	All my written communications are clear and concise.			
7	I ask a colleague to check important documents that I write.			
8	I never use written communication if I can speak to the person concerned.			
9	People understand what I mean when I send them things that I have written.			
10	I think writing a report is something I could do without problems.			

Listening Skills

One of the most important parts of communication is listening to what other people have to say. If you don't, you will miss out on crucial pieces of information. This information may be about things that are going wrong, things that are preventing the team from performing at their best, or ideas and suggestions that can improve the way that things are done. In other cases people may ask for advice or support. If you don't listen, all of this will be lost and as a result the motivation of the team and their performance will be much lower than it could be.

"Listening" is not as easy as it sounds. To be fully concentrating on what the other person is saying and to make sure that you fully understand what they mean requires effort and practice. Many people assume that they know what someone means as soon as they have heard the first couple of sentences. How often have you heard someone say – "Oh yes, I know what you mean..." – before you have had the chance to get your whole message across. Bear in mind that often the most important piece of information comes at the end. Make sure you do not interrupt.

	Question	usually	sometimes	seldom
1	I maintain eye contact with the speaker when listening.			
2	The speaker's appearance and the style and quality of their delivery greatly affect whether I think what they have to say is worthwhile.			
3	I try to align my thoughts and feelings with those of the speaker.			
4	I listen for specific facts rather than the "big picture".			
5	I listen for both factual content and the emotion behind the literal words.			

How Did You Score?

Questions 2, 4, 9, 10		Questions 1, 3, 5, 6, 7, 8	
Usually	1 point	Usually	3 points
Sometimes	2 points	Sometimes	2 points
Seldom	3 points	Seldom	1 point

More than 27

Your listening skills seem to be good, but there may be room for improvement in some areas.

22–26

You have some skills, but you could achieve considerable improvements.

Under 22

Your skills need substantial improvement in many areas.

	Question	usually	sometimes	seldom
6	I ask questions for clarification.			
7	I withold judgement of what the speaker has said until he or she has finished.			
8	I make a conscious effort to evaluate the logic and consistency of what is being said.			
9	While listening I think about what I am going to say as soon as I have my chance.			
10	I prefer to be the last person to speak.			

Discussing Problems And Getting Agreement

t is important when discussing difficult subjects that you do not lose sight of the core issues and the need to reach a resolution. There is a tendency in some organizations for team leaders to impose agreement on other people – "So that's what we've agreed then" – when in fact that is what the leader has just decided. This imposition of one person's view is counterproductive. Agreement means that everyone involved accepts the decision. It is probably not very often that a boss says to someone on their team "It's not critical what I think, but it's critical what you think of this because you are going to be the one doing the job". Getting real agreement can be both difficult and time consuming, but the benefit is that you have everybody working at full potential towards the same goals, rather than half-heartedly towards different goals.

Attempts to coerce other people into doing what you want may end in short-term success, but it always results in long-term failure – agreement should be reached by mutual consent, not by intimidation.

	Question	usually	sometimes	seldom
1	I state my position at once and then invite discussion.			
2	I always look for a mutually beneficial outcome.			
3	I never back away from a good argument.			
4	I help the other person to understand how to solve their problem even if it takes time.			
5	I try to understand other people's views.			
6	People come to me with their problems.			

How Did You Score?

Questions 1, 3, 7, 9, 10, 12		Questions 2, 4, 5, 6, 8, 11	
Usually	1 point	Usually	3 points
Sometimes	2 points	Sometimes	2 points
Seldom	3 points	Seldom	1 point

More than 32
Your negotiating skills seem to be good, but there may be room for improvement in some areas.

26–32
You have some skills, but you could achieve considerable improvements.

Under 26
Your skills need substantial improvement in many areas.

	Question	usually	sometimes	seldom
7	I tell people what their problems are.			
8	I always stick to facts and events and never insult the other person.			
9	I am prepared to give in totally rather than force someone else to change their mind.			
10	I always put any controversial issues to one side to avoid problems.			
11	I let the other person explain their position first.			
12	I let the other person have their way if they start getting emotional.			

3

Getting it right
Basic principles
Preparation
Delivery

How does communication work?

How can I prepare my message?

Was my message understood?

How Communication Works

Communication has been successful if the message that is received is the same as the one that was sent. This simple model shows all of the factors which can affect the communication process. In the model the message is sent by a sender to a receiver (who could be either an individual or a group). Of course the roles can switch during the course of a conversation as the receiver replies and becomes the sender. The model shows that communication can be complex.

Encoding and transmitting the message

Encoding is taking what you want to say and presenting it in a way that the receiver will understand. You use the transmitters – the senses of hearing, seeing, touching – to communicate. Try listening to someone talking to you when your eyes are closed – this shows how much non-verbal signals contribute to understanding messages. Even if you say that you are interested, by looking bored or repeatedly checking your watch, you send other signals.

They Work Out What You Mean & Reply

They Receive
Receptors   Decoding

They Send

Channels (Messages)

Meaning

Encoding

Transmitter

Transmitters

NOISE

Channels (Messages)

Encoding

Receptors

Meaning

Decoding

You Send

You Receive

YOU WANT TO SEND A MESSAGE

The message moves into the communication channels

Note the noise area between the sender and receiver that may impact upon the message. Noise can be any background distraction, such as workmen or someone talking. It can also be a distraction which does not make an actual sound, such as something on your mind that affects your concentration. These are all things that can prevent a receiver understanding the message as the sender intended. Remember the last conversation you tried to have next to a busy major road or in a noisy car, or think of the times when you have tried to have a telephone conversation at the same time as doing some paperwork. The noise probably made getting your message across much more difficult than it would normally have been. You need to minimize this noise by removing or reducing all distractions that may impair the ability of the receiver to focus on your message. It is not only the message that is important, but where and how it is delivered.

Arriving at the receptors

The senses of the receiver are important because they are the receptors that take in the message. Are they listening and watching? Are they paying attention? Are they tuned-in to receiving a message? Are they listening for the critical parts of the message? Have you ever noticed that someone you are talking to is nodding as you speak, but clearly not paying attention? You probably wonder whether they are thinking about your message, or what they will be doing at the weekend. Also, people with disabilities who may have lost the use of sight, hearing or other receptors, need you to make a special effort to make sure that they can understand your message. For example, someone who can't see very well will not pick up your non-verbal signals (your hand gestures and smile).

Decoding

Each receiver will decode the message according to their own perceptions, not those of the sender, and will interpret the message in a unique way. If there is a difference in perception, there will be confusion. Consider the potential problems when communicating with a large group. Have you ever been to a meeting where you and other people have heard the same words, but later disagreed on what was actually said, or what was meant by the words? When preparing your message, try to consider the different ways that it could be interpreted by the people receiving it. For example, if your boss were to announce that "there are a lot of changes coming up", some people may see it as a threat, others as an opportunity.

Why on earth bother with this complex process?
How often have you heard at work
"*Oh…that's what you meant, I thought you wanted me to …*" or, "*No, no I didn't mean that… I meant this…*"
Understanding the model allows you to make sure that your message gets through and helps you avoid those problems that may arise.

The First Steps To Effective Communication

Getting your message across is not as simple as it may sound at first. It is up to the sender to make sure that the receiver gets the message and that the message received matches the one that was sent. Lots of factors contribute to even the most simple forms of communication and many problems can arise. If the message does not get through, it is probably the fault of the sender. For example, if the receiver forgets to switch on their fax machine, it is still the sender's fault if the message does not get through, because the sender should have checked by telephone that the fax has arrived.

How the message is worded has a great impact on how it is received and understood. For example, "Write out the sales figures NOW !" or "Peter, would you please write out the latest sales figures for me?" say different things.

THE STAGES OF EFFECTIVE COMMUNICATION

- You construct the message
- You match the message to the receiver
- You prepare the receiver
- You send the message
- They receive the message
- They interpret the message
- You confirm the message has been understood

EXERCISE
Sometimes even though we have given the right information the other person still misunderstands – who is at fault? Describe a swing hanging from a tree branch to another person. Do not use the word "swing" and do not mention what a swing is designed to do. Ask the other person to draw what you are describing. It is unlikely that the finished picture will look like the swing that you had in your imagination.

The content of the message is crucial. Consider whether the message in the example conveys everything that is needed? Does Peter write out the sales figures by area or by product? Does he write them in ascending or descending order and should he use some kind of graphical representation ?

The means by which the message is delivered – face-to-face, on the telephone, or as a memo – will also affect the result that the message has on the receiver. Evidence suggests that in most communication, particularly verbal, the first delivery of a message is usually only 50 percent successful, so there is plenty of room for improvement. Written communication has the advantage of being open to less misinterpretation, but how many times have you "skim read" a document and not really understood the message it contains, got the wrong message, or had to re-read or seek further clarification?

Perception and understanding
All too often we assume that other people share our experiences, perceptions and views. Unfortunately this is not the case and the perceptions of the audience will affect the way that they interpret your message. To communicate effectively it is important to make sure that the receiver understands your perceptions about a message as well as

the message itself. If someone likes you, they will take the message on board. If not, they may ignore it! The receiver may not view the matter in the same way as you. You may think that doing the sales figures is an important job – someone else may think that it is tedious. Ensure that the receiver understands your perception. Take account of the difference between your perception and theirs and draw attention to it. You might say, "I know you don't think that preparing the sales figures is important, but it is essential that it is done for my team to be able to operate effectively, and we think that it's very important."

Everyone is different

Quickly jot down the swing that you were describing in the exercise on the previous page. Is this the only way that it could be imagined? Ask a couple of people to do the same exercise and compare their pictures with yours and the illustrations (right). No doubt they all look at least slightly different. Each of us has unique associations and experiences which determine exactly how we think about things; even something as simple as a swing in a tree.

This has implications for the message and how it is delivered. Explain your perceptions as part of the message to avoid confusion. Do not assume that the receiver will "get your drift".

There are three stages in sending a successful message

1 preparation

2 delivery

3 confirmation of understanding

It is often said that many drafts end up being the final message. Allow yourself enough time to structure and match your message so that it is in a form that will make it easy for the receiver to understand. Some messages will not take long to fine tune to match the receiver – for example, if you are giving a simple message to someone who you know. Others need careful preparation – for example if you are giving a long message to a group of your seniors. In cases such as this, allow yourself plenty of time to prepare your message.

Preparing The Message

I keep six honest serving menThey taught me all I knew Their names are What and Why and When, and How and Where and Who

Rudyard Kipling

Careful construction of the message and matching its form and delivery to the audience is critical for success. Do not neglect this stage of communication. Good preparation will make sure the delivery goes smoothly and will ensure that you avoid any barriers to your message being caused by a receiver who is not prepared to receive a message, or an incomplete or inaccurate message that does not match the receiver. Whether you are preparing a study on a complex subject or a quick briefing for a simple task, the principles are the same.

Constructing the initial message

Put together the message that you want to send so that you achieve the objective you want. So the first question is "What do I want to achieve?" For example, is it to get a specific job done? to brief a group on the plans for next year? or to talk over performance problems with a team member?

The message itself can be structured with the help of Rudyard Kipling's poem *Six Honest Serving Men* (left); a poem that everyone should know if they have to plan anything. Try to memorize it if you can. It will prove very useful in any number of areas.

Using this format ensures that all of the critical information is included. The structure is simple, ask youself what you want to achieve, why it needs to be done, when it needs to be done by, how it can best be achieved, where it needs to happen and who needs to do it. This method is shown by the examples opposite, where it has been used to plan some typical work messages.

Hopefully your version, based on the suggested format, will have been similar. You may need to add more detail if the receiver needs it. It may be useful to give details on what the problems were. Read what you have written and think about whether your version would have got the message across successfully.

TELLING YOUR TEAM ABOUT THE NEW PRODUCTS BEING LAUNCHED

You can apply the format suggested by the poem to constructing a message:

WHAT do I want to achieve? **I want to inform the team about the new products.**

WHY does it need to be done? **Because they need to know what is coming up so as to ensure that on the launch of the new products they will be able to answer client questions.**

WHEN does it need to be done by? **They need to be aware now and fully conversant by January next year.**

HOW is it best done? **They have initial knowledge now and will need to read briefing sheets which are due out next month.**

WHERE? **There will be an initial presentation in the training room – then they should do the rest of their preparation in their own time outside work.**

WHO by? **All team members need to be fully conversant with all new products.**

SO WHAT IS THE FINAL MESSAGE ?

   "You all need to know about these new products so you can answer client questions. I'm letting you know now so that you have time to read up on them and be conversant by next January. The briefing sheets will be out next month."

YOU NEED TO DISCUSS A PERFORMANCE PROBLEM WITH KATHERINE, ONE OF YOUR TEAM

You can apply the same format to constructing a message for one-to-one communications:

WHAT DO I NEED TO ACHIEVE? **An improvement in Katherine's performance.**

WHY DOES IT NEED TO BE DONE? **Because her performance is not as good as I need for the team to be effective. There are problems with her technical skills.**

WHEN DOES IT NEED TO BE DONE BY? **As soon as possible.**

HOW IS IT BEST DONE? **By agreeing steps and targets to improve her performance.**

WHERE? **At work and possibly with the help of a training course.**

WHO by? **A partnership between her and me.**

SO WHAT IS THE FINAL MESSAGE ?

Write down what you think the message would be then compare it to the suggested one below:

   "Katherine, you need to improve some of your technical skills to allow the team to be effective. We need to do this as soon as possible and we will agree steps and targets in partnership to achieve this, possibly sending you on a training course."

...What you say should be simple, clear and to the point...

Matching The Message To The Receiver

Once you have decided what you need to say, the next step is to fine tune the message to match the audience. Each message that you send has to be tuned into the receiver. For example, you would not talk to a group of your colleagues in the same way as you would to a group of 11 year olds. You need to think about exactly how you will get your message across to the audience. Which words will you use? Are technical words suitable? Does your audience already sympathize with your viewpoint or do you have to convince them?

Do you have to get the message over to one of your team, the board of your organization, a colleague in an office on the other side of the world, or a group of strangers who you have not met before? Even within your own team there may be a difference in the way you need to get your message across.

The two areas that need to be considered when trying to match the message to the audience are information and delivery style.

Information Try to match the level of information in the message to the needs of the receiver. The amount of detail depends on how much the receiver already knows about the subject. There is an important link to delegation if the message is about the receiver doing something on your behalf.

Compare how you would get the same job done by a senior and experienced colleague and how you would brief an inexperienced trainee ? The objective – getting the job done – is the same, but you would need to include more information for the inexperienced trainee. He or she would need to be told how to do the job and the background – why it needs to be done. The experienced colleague would know this already.

Delivery style Do you take a quiet step-by-step approach – checking the understanding of the receiver at each stage? Alternatively, do you give the receiver a fast and furious delivery? Do you use lots of practical examples, or concentrate on the theory?

When speaking try to achieve a friendly tone that is clear and matched to the listener. Again you can probably think of individuals who you work with to whom you would deliver the same message in different ways.

To help match the message to the receiver these are some of the questions you may find helpful to ask yourself. Although the questions in the chart below refer to "them" this matching process is just as important when dealing with individuals as groups. *All* of these questions apply just as much to communications with individuals as to those with groups.

Who is receiving the message?	What is their perception of you?
Why are they there?	What do they want from you? What do you want from them?
What do they know about the subject?	Will this limit the use of technical words? Will they understand the concepts? Will they know if you get things wrong? Are they more expert, less expert or on the same level as you?
What is their link to you?	Are they more senior, your team, peers or people you've not met before?
Are they on your side or do you have to win them over?	
Are there those who will have difficulty with technical phrases?	
Are there non-English speakers?	What is their level of English? Will this limit the words you can use? Will you need to learn the key phrases in another language?
How big is the audience?	The larger the audience the more impersonal the communication process becomes and the more important it is to "get them on your side". This is especially true if they don't know you.
How formal is the message ?	Some messages, such as presentations to seniors, are very formal.

Deciding On The Means Of Delivery

Think about written information sources you use at work, such as handbooks. They have the advantage that you can dip into them at the place and time you want. But remember written messages can be lost!

You can deliver your message either verbally or in writing. Verbal delivery includes: presentations, one-to-one, team meetings, and by telephone. Written delivery includes: letter, report, e-mail or memo. Select the one that gets the message over as effectively as possible and maximizes the ability of the receiver to understand it as you intended. But bear in mind that the means you use to get it across will also send a secondary message – "If he thought it was really that important he should have put it in writing", or, "She could have spoken to me about it rather than sending me an e-mail". Do not forget this aspect of how you send the message.

Delivery mechanics This addresses the means of delivering the message from the purely technical perspective. If the message is more complex and difficult for the receiver to remember, or will require large amounts of note taking, then a written message may be more

WHEN TRYING TO DECIDE WHICH METHOD OF DELIVERY IS BEST SUITED TO A PARTICULAR SITUATION ASK YOURSELF THE FOLLOWING QUESTIONS

1   Do I need a record of what happened?

2   Is the volume/complexity of information so great that the receiver will be unable to take it all in at one time?

3   Do I want the receiver to be able to respond at once to my message?

4   Do I want the receiver to be able to think about the message and respond at a later date?

5   How many people do I want to get the message? Is it the same message for all of them?

6   Do I want to be able to change, add to or fine tune the message as I deliver it?

7   Is it a formal or informal message?

8   Am I unable to contact the receiver verbally or is it very difficult to do so?

9   Are there geographical or physical restrictions on the means I can use?

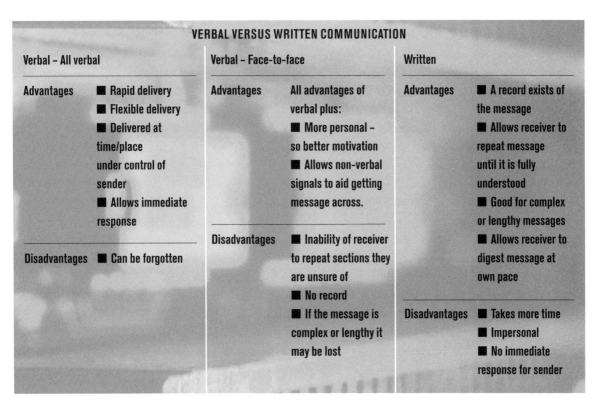

VERBAL VERSUS WRITTEN COMMUNICATION

Verbal – All verbal		Verbal – Face-to-face		Written	
Advantages	■ Rapid delivery ■ Flexible delivery ■ Delivered at time/place under control of sender ■ Allows immediate response	Advantages	All advantages of verbal plus: ■ More personal – so better motivation ■ Allows non-verbal signals to aid getting message across.	Advantages	■ A record exists of the message ■ Allows receiver to repeat message until it is fully understood ■ Good for complex or lengthy messages ■ Allows receiver to digest message at own pace
Disadvantages	■ Can be forgotten	Disadvantages	■ Inability of receiver to repeat sections they are unsure of ■ No record ■ If the message is complex or lengthy it may be lost	Disadvantages	■ Takes more time ■ Impersonal ■ No immediate response for sender

effective. Written messages also provide a record of the message and allow the receiver to refer back to the original. The receiver has the opportunity to digest the information over time and in the order that suits them. This is crucial if you expect a response from your audience – they need time to think and consider.

Verbal messages are more personal – especially when delivered face-to-face. They allow immediate response and faster development of ideas or solutions than written ones. Verbal messages are more effective for the fast communication of simple messages, but they can also be forgotten easily.

In some circumstances both verbal and written messages are necessary. For example, when ordering office supplies you may need to make a telephone call and follow this up with a faxed confirmation. A verbal account of a forthcoming meeting may need to be followed by a written agenda. The written message will reinforce the verbal message, boosting the perception of the message's priority in the eyes of the person receiving it.

Getting The Delivery Right

Think carefully about the message you want to get over. Would it help the receiver if they were prepared in advance? If it could be helpful, do it.

The most obvious choice of a mechanical delivery method won't necessarily give the best impression to the receiver. For example, your annual performance appraisal could be faxed to you quickly and effectively, but what would you think of this means of delivery? You would probably feel that this is the sort of matter that really should be dealt with face-to-face. In general terms, if a message is to have a personal impact on the receiver, then it needs to be delivered verbally, preferably face-to-face and if this is not possible, on the telephone.

The message is more than the words

The non-verbal signals you send via your physical stance in face-to-face communication also send a message. For example, a smile will make the receiver feel relaxed. Try to lean towards the other person during the communication process and maintain eye contact to give the receiver confidence that you are sincere in what you are saying.

If you are receiving a message, you can also accidentally give off the wrong signals. For example, if you look around at the room while someone is talking to you this will certainly be interpreted by the sender as boredom on your part.

Rehearse the delivery

Because you need to get the message right you should practice it where possible. This is particularly important if the message is to be delivered face-to-face. You may think that it is obvious that you practice addressing a group, but surely there is no need to rehearse a one-on-one encounter? But why shouldn't you? If the message is important, you may find that if you say it as you first intend, it may not sound right. Try to get another person to listen to you as you practice – this may give you another perspective on how it sounds – or how it could be misunderstood.

If your message is in writing, it may seem that it is not possible to practice your delivery. But reading it through is good practice. Check that the message makes sense, even if you have to read out the letter or memo to yourself. In haste you may find that you use the wrong words or fail to get the message right. Again, you may find that letting another person check over what you have written is a wise precaution. It is easy to miss your own mistakes in a written document because your brain will automatically "correct" them as you read. However, this still leaves the mistakes on the paper.

Doing The Support Work

You have now prepared your message and practiced the delivery, so all you have to do is deliver it to the receiver. But where and when? Are you briefed, in case the receiver asks questions? Have you got all the equipment that you need? You need to check that the correct resources are in place to ensure an effective delivery of the message. This is particularly important if you have a more formal message to get over, but you can also apply this advice to informal day-to-day communication.

Plan to deliver the message at an appropriate time and in an appropriate place. If you need to get an important message across, make an appointment and, if necessary, put it in your diary. This will avoid interruptions during the meeting. Also, by planning an appropriate time and place you will be able to prepare what you are going to say, so you will be more relaxed and the whole tone of the message will improve. This will reduce distraction and noise that may blunt your message. For example, it would be better to discuss an employee's poor performance in a private room rather than in the main office. Consider whether you will have to fix a time in advance with the receiver.

If you are giving a presentation or chairing a meeting, check that any equipment that you need, for example seating, a chart, an overhead projector, or refreshments are there. Check that everything works. There is nothing quite as embarassing as turning on the overhead projector at a critical point in a meeting to find out that it doesn't work. It also disrupts the flow of the meeting and blunts your message.

Make sure that you have read everything that you need to and that any paperwork that is necessary has been completed. Bring any handouts or reference material that you will need with you, and paper and a pen if you will need to make notes as you go along.

If you have to read from notes, the message is probably a complicated one and your audience may wish to take notes. If you haven't warned them beforehand to bring a pen and paper then you should provide them. There is no point in clearly explaining a complex message if it is later forgotten. You can make sure that everyone has all of the critical information by providing pre-prepared notes. These can include background information, which is not covered in your message, but which may be of value to the audience.

The more important the communication the more time you should allow to check it.

Doing The Support Work

SUPPORT CHECKLIST

1 Venue
Choose where you intend to deliver the message. Does it need booking? Do you need to tell the receiver?

2 Equipment
Do you need overheads, handouts or other equipment to help you get the message over? Will they need to take notes?
Refreshments

3 Timing
How long will you need to get across your message? When will you do it?
This applies not only to presenting to a large audience, but also to most other forms of communication. Have you made sure you that you will not be disturbed?

4 Paperwork
Have you read all of the related papers? Have you got all the supporting documents? Will you need to take notes?

5 Yourself
As well as checking your resources it is worth making sure that you are covered by your preliminary preparation as well. Arriving late and looking untidy sends a message to the other person – you can't be bothered to arrive on time or you can't organize yourself to arrive on time – so how important is your message? Any rush, confusion or stress will distract you from getting your message across in the best possible way.
Try to arrive five minutes early to check that everything is in place and to relax.

Preparing The Receiver

Ensure that the receiver or audience are going to give their full attention to your message. If it is important, give them plenty of advance warning that you are about to deliver the message. In most day-to-day communication the preparation of the receiver happens immediately before you give them your message. For example you might say, "John could I please have a word with you about…" or "I think that this is an important issue that we need to discuss". But in some cases, such as team briefings, meetings or complex discussions and appraisals, more warning is needed. This is especially important if you expect the receiver to respond in detail to any points or questions that you have. He or she will need to do preparation work before the meeting.

If a team meeting is due, alert the team verbally and then confirm the time, date and location in writing. If you want to discuss something with an individual, let them know beforehand. In many cases the communication may also need a response from the other person. Advance warning gives them time to put together their own responses or thoughts, or to gather the information that they need to give you. If both sender and receiver have prepared themselves beforehand, both will get much more benefit from the communication.

SUMMARY
Using the "What, why, when, where, how and who" format can make the whole preparation process easier. Consider the case study on page 37, *Telling the team about new products being launched.* This is how the message could have been planned using Kipling's poem.

I need to tell the team about the new products within the next week via a face-to-face meeting with discussion. I need to book a room with an overhead projector. It will probably take 90 minutes and I will issue notes about the new products at the end. I may need someone from the production team to answer any technical questions that come up so I must contact them in advance.

The preparation phase has now put all the foundations in place to ensure that the delivery of the message goes smoothly. If you have got the preparation right, the actual delivery will probably go without any problems.

Delivering Your Message

If your boss says, "You are the most professional person I have ever worked with", in a genuine way, it can boost your confidence greatly. But if it is said sarcastically, it can destroy your confidence. Though the same words are used, the meaning is exactly opposite. So think carefully about the tone of delivery that you use and make sure that it supports what you want to say.

Getting the receiver's attention and giving notice of your intention to communicate well in advance may be appropriate for some situations such as a meeting, but for most day-to-day communications, such as telling someone the answer to a query that they raised with you, do this immediately before you deliver your message. For example you might say "Here is the answer to your query John. The sales fell by 20 percent last month."

Prepare the receiver for the main message by following five steps outlined below. The method can be applied in a range of situations, from giving a presentation to a large number of people, to passing on a piece of information on the telephone. The preparation sets the stage for the main message so that the receiver is ready and willing to receive it.

1 Check the receiver is ready to receive the message and to give feedback Even though the receiver is present you need to make sure that they are ready to receive the message. You should have made sure that the time and place are appropriate for the delivery of the message, but there may be other immediate distractions that may prevent communication being successful – so double check that the receiver is relaxed and listening for your message.

2 Outline what the message is about Set the scene for the receiver – it is useful to give him or her a brief outline of what you intend to cover in your message. This outline has exactly the same function as the executive summary in a report or the introduction to a presentation.

3 Background Put the communication in context for the receiver. Give him or her the background. For example, tell your assistant that you need him to pay attention to the presentation of the report that he is preparing because there has recently been a memo to all managers about badly presented work.

4 Say why the information is important to you This is confirmation of your assumptions and perceptions. It establishes why you are sending the message to them and your thoughts or attitudes about it. This makes sure that they interpret the message from your perspective. The receiver may disagree with your viewpoint, but at least they will understand what it is. Many people forget the importance of this. If the message doesn't include how you view the issue, as important or urgent for example, the receiver may not respond as you want. Getting across your perception is critical.

5 Say why the information will benefit the receiver In any communication the receiver needs to have some motivation to take on board the message. You should try to bear this in mind all the time. Think about when you tell one of your team that they have to do a job. If you point out how the job will benefit them – for example by enabling them to gain experience or by getting to know more about a certain area – this improves their motivation, both to listen to the message and to do the job.

Delivering the message Now you have decided on the most effective means for delivery you need to make the delivery to the best of your ability.

If you have chosen to use the spoken word to deliver your message, make sure that you use an appropriate tone and that your body language is backing up your message. These factors are just as important as the words themselves. Keep eye contact and speak clearly, with confidence and in a friendly tone. Speak up, be direct, be specific. Avoid "ummm" and "er" and cut out any unnecessary detail or waffle. If it is appropriate, smile as you speak to put the receiver at ease. Be sincere. Do not talk too fast and check that the receiver is keeping up. If the message is verbal, watch and listen to see that the receiver appears to be taking it in. Are they acknowledging your points? agreeing with you? showing interest? With a telephone message you have to listen for these signals. If you feel that the receiver may be getting confused then stop and ask them if they understand. Rephrase the point if necessary. The more complex the message, the more often you need to check that the receiver has understood. Usually you are building up to a conclusion that contains the critical part of the message and it is essential that the receiver has understood the steps that have taken you there.

Do not forget that getting feedback can apply to situations where people may be more experienced or knowledgeable than you. They can give you information or advice that will help you do your job better. "What do you think of this proposal?" can get valuable information for you and show your respect for the individual.

Has Your Message Been Understood?

People do not use
the feedback
loop because:
■ they think that
because they
understand their
own message
everyone else will
■ they have not got
time to check that the
audienceunderstands
■ they do not want
to suggest to the
audience that they
were not listening

This feedback stage is the most often forgotten part of the communication process, yet it is of critical importance. It is the last chance to check that the message has been understood before things start to happen, and potentially start to go wrong. This is true, not only if you have asked people to do things, but also if you have given them information. Their views, opinions and plans are being formed the moment you stop communicating and if you do not check that the message has got through properly, those views, opinions and plans may not be what you intended.

To make sure that your message was understood as you intended, get feedback from the receiver by asking questions and listening to the answers.

The very least you need to do is to ask if there are any questions, but use both active listening *and* questioning as often as possible to make sure that your message has got through.

In the basic communication model on page 32 the "feedback loop" is where the sender asks the receiver to confirm the message, in order to see if it matches the message sent. However, simply asking "do you understand" may not always tell you if there has been genuine understanding. People tend to say what they think others want to hear, especially at work, because they are afraid that admitting that they do not understand may make them appear to be stupid. Also, a person may think that they have understood what you meant, but have totally misunderstood your point. So ask the other person to tell you what they think your message is. You need to ask questions, but do not forget to listen to the answers. If the message is anything other than very simple, you may find it more effective to work in stages – after each important point confirm that the receiver has understood.

With written messages, we all assume that the receiver will come back to us if they are unsure or unhappy, but this doesn't often happen. If you have given a written message there is nothing to stop you verbally checking that it has been understood, just as you would in conversation. Try to do this where possible to make sure that the receiver does raise any concerns. Because it has been put in writing, he or she may feel that you are not interested in their view.

MOST CLOSED QUESTIONS CAN BE QUITE EASILY TURNED INTO OPEN QUESTIONS

Closed question – "do you think this plan is ok?"

Open question – "What problems do you feel might occur if we use this plan?"

Questions This is of importance at all times, not just when you want to send a message and check understanding, but at any time you need to check what other people think. Use questions in all situations to check how effective your communication has been. As a check to whether your message has got through just ask the receiver what they thought you were trying to say or what they thought of your message.

Asking open questions (questions that don't have a "yes" or "no" answer) is a good way to get a response from someone who is reluctant to give feedback. Open questions usually start with the words "how, what, when, where, why" – which often encourage a response and cannot generally be answered with a simple "yes" or "no". These make the receiver give you more feedback than just "yes" or "no", which helps you decide whether they have really understood.

Active listening If you ask a question, you need to listen to the answer. All of it. Allow the person who you asked the question time to compose their answer and allow them the opportunity to give it all to you before you speak again.

As you listen try to support the person who is talking – confirming that you understand by nodding as they speak. If they have difficulty, try to help them phrase what they want to say – but check with them as you do this. For example, you might ask, "so, are you telling me that you are not very happy with the new holiday timetable that has been drawn up for the Christmas break?" At the end of a response to a question confirm that you have correctly understood what has been said by paraphrasing and ask them to confirm that you have received and understood the message correctly. For more details on active listening, see page 59.

Write down three recent events when something went wrong at work. At which stage do you think the problem occurred? For example, did the initial message leave out vital information that you needed, or was the failure one of interpretation? For each case jot down a few notes about how the problem could have been avoided. This will have enabled you to identify some of the barriers to communication that can occur.

Barriers To Communications

Barriers that prevent your message getting through can have disastrous results. For example, if a faulty telephone line resulted in a client being unable to get through when they needed to, a valuable sale might be lost. Watch out for barriers preventing the message getting through each time you communicate. Some of the barriers may be your fault, some the fault of technology, but they are rarely the fault of the person who is receiving the message. Barriers can arise at each stage of the communication process.

	Stage	Barrier	Example	Solution
1	Constructing the message	The message was incomplete	You forgot to give the deadline for a piece of work	Make sure the message contains all the information needed and accurately reflects what you mean
		The message was inaccurate, you did not express what you really meant to	You said that you would like to have "a chat some time soon" when you really wanted "an urgent meeting"	
2	Matching the message	The message was not "tuned" into the audience that was to receive it. This applies just as much to communicating to one person as to a group	You used too many technical words for a non-technical audience	Make sure the message is matched to the receiver – by adjusting the level of information, and style and tone of delivery. Add information about your perceptions if the receiver's perceptions are likely to be different
			You used a tone that was unsympathetic to the audience	
			You spoke too fast	
3	Preparing the receiver	The receiver was not ready to accept the message	The receiver was not expecting a message; they were busy with another task and were not paying attention	Make sure the message is delivered away from distractions and that the receiver is ready to receive before starting to deliver the message

	Stage	Barrier	Example	Solution
4	Sending the message	The means by which the message was sent was inappropriate	A long and complicated fax could have been replaced effectively by a five minute face-to-face briefing	Make sure the means of delivery is appropriate to the message – ask yourself if you would like to have this message delivered to you in this way?
5	Receiving the message	There was some problem in the arrival of the message	The receiver was off ill for a day and missed the message; The e-mail was delayed by a computer failure	Ensure that the means of delivery will get the message to the right place at the right time. If necessary confirm the delivery – things can go missing. When communicating face-to-face minimize distractions
6	Interpreting the message	The message is not understood as intended	You did not tell the receiver that something was important because you thought it was obvious, but the receiver had a different idea of what was important	Try to understand the perceptions and assumptions of the receiver. Feed this into the "matching the message" process and include information on your perceptions
7	Confirmation of message	Failure to seek or listen to feedback – no confirmation of the message being correctly received	You did not check that the receiver understood and as a result the receiver did not get the job done on time	Always check the message the receiver has received via feedback – using questions and listening. This is your last chance to make sure your message has got across as you intended before things start to happen

4

Face-to-face
Telephone
Feedback
Written word

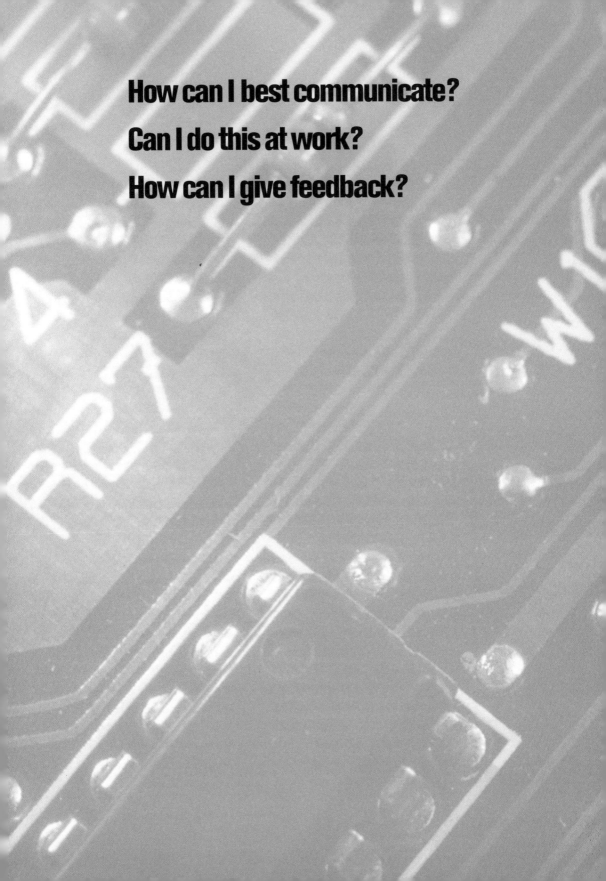

How can I best communicate?

Can I do this at work?

How can I give feedback?

Getting It Right At Work

You need to build on your current skills. This chapter looks at the situations that come up most often at work and provides you with strategies that you can use immediately to make your communication more effective. The main areas covered are one-to-one communication, group meetings, written communication and telephone communication.

Face-to-face with another person

Discussing an issue face-to-face can save time. A meeting allows you to put across complex ideas. A one-to-one situation means that you are on the spot, ready to deal with any questions and problems there and then. This type of communication can also have a great motivational effect on your team members. You have the opportunity to fully involve the other person in the subject under discussion. This means that all those involved fully understand what they need to do and why.

By talking to people face-to-face you will also be able to maintain the initiative. You will be able to anticipate and dispel rumours and hearsay before they begin. Although it may sometimes be tempting to allow things to drift remember that it is better for people to be kept informed about developments and decisions, even if they are not happy about them.

Prepare yourself well before you talk to someone face-to-face. Before you begin make sure that you have clarified the following points in your own mind:

- What is the message about?
- What is the background to the message?
- Why is it important to you?
- Why is it important to the receiver?
- Why is it important to the company?
- How will the message be of benefit to the receiver?

KEEP IMPROVING
In the wide variety of situations that you may face at work there is no simple answer to getting it right. Keep referring back to the basic format of communication to give you a logical process to produce the right message and guidance on the basic steps to effective delivery. Then "fine tune" your methods using the following sections which cover the main different areas of communication encountered in the work place so that it matches the situation and the individual or group involved.

CASE STUDY

You would like John to be in charge of opening a new branch office in Paris.
He has the management skills and experience, and can speak fluent French.

WHAT DO I WANT TO ACHIEVE? **To get John to open and run the new Paris office.**

WHY DOES IT NEED TO BE DONE? **The Paris office has to open and he is the best candidate.**

WHEN DOES IT NEED TO HAPPEN? **The office has to be open by next October.**

HOW IS IT BEST DONE? **By releasing John from his current post in 3 months time in order to
concentrate on preparation for the Paris opening.**

WHERE? **London and Paris.**

WHO? **John and some administrative support.**

Note down the message components:
    John to run the new Paris office
    Best candidate
    Opening on 1st October next year
    He can be released to start in Paris in 3 months time
    Based London/Paris
    Administration support will be provided
    Ask for confirmation and get feedback

The final message is:
"John, as you know there is to be a new office in Paris from the end of next year. This will be a
first step in our expansion into Europe – so it is very important that it is successful. Because
of your experience and fluent French I'd like you to run it. This is obviously a very good
opportunity for you to advance your career and help develop the company. You can start work
in three months and will get administrative support. What are your views on this offer?"

*...Aggressiveness
does not win
the help and
cooperation
of others...*

Face-to-Face With A Group

Many managers shy away from speaking to their team as a group although they are happy to speak to them as individuals! Do you prefer to deal with people individually even if the information that you want to convey is common to all of them? Do you try to avoid a meeting by putting up a memo on the notice board? Though putting up a memo gets your message across it is only effective for the most simple messages and if there is any chance that the people concerned want to ask questions or seek further explanation it is not effective.

This type of communication involves talking to the people who you work with on a daily basis. However, it can also apply to giving a presentation or speaking to a group of strangers. The principles are the same. Speaking face-to-face with a group is easier and more efficient than giving the same information to everyone individually and it ensures that everyone gets the same message. Face-to-face communication has the advantage that it allows the receivers to respond immediately.

The general principles of briefings and holding team meetings are covered in this section. Formal presentations are not dealt with specifically here, but the same principles apply as when speaking to any group of people.

Briefing the team When giving instructions to a team or individual many managers often leave out critical information. By following the format below you will ensure that all of the important information is included in your message. Before the start of the briefing make sure that you have done all of the necessary preliminary preparations.

BRIEFING THE TEAM	
Background	Tell the team why the task is necessary
Objectives	Outline what the team or group is aiming to achieve
General Tasks	Let the team know the overall plan
Specific tasks	Detail the stages, individual tasks and objectives involved
Administration	Tell everyone where support is coming from, resources, interim reports, action on problems, contacts
Timings	Outline the start time, finish and intermediate stages or deadlines
Any questions?	Don't miss out the crucial feedback stage

Team meetings Meetings may be called regularly, or on an ad-hoc basis to deal with particular situations. Expect more team involvement. Also a number of messages will probably need to be put across and discussed. The structure of the meeting must allow for discussion. Getting your team meetings to run smoothly is very important. Badly run team meetings are one of the most common sources of wasted time in organizations. The following format should help you ensure that your meetings are well run and get the message across, resulting in improved team motivation.

Leading the meeting In some cases the team meeting is an opportunity for you to give information, for example if you need to explain plans for the future. Alternatively, a meeting may be used to gather information, for example if a group of employees want you to pass on some ideas or concerns to the boss.

As a group leader make sure that everyone gets the opportunity to get their message across.

In your organization there may be no formal system, such as a regular team briefing, for this type of exchange of information up and down the management structure, but you can run them for your team.

TEAM MEETINGS

Set the stage	Give advance notice of time and place Do your preliminary preparation
Prepare the message	Group the points that you wish to make Make the information relevant to the audience Review the team's performance (if applicable) Try to anticipate any questions
Get their attention	Tell everyone what the meeting is about Outline the background of the subject under discussion Explain why the message is important to you, them and the organization Explain how it will benefit them
Deliver the message	Explain your message, the problem or matter to be discussed
Ask for feedback	Let the team contribute their views
Control the meeting	Don't allow side discussions Allow only one person to talk at once If you ask for views, get them from everyone Avoid distractions Support your boss
Summarize	Sum up what has been agreed Detail what is to be done by who and by when Look forward to the next meeting

Follow up – After the meeting a written version of your summary will ensure that what has been agreed, what is to be done, by who and by when is available to all. This will ensure that it gets done.

Getting Effective Feedback

FEEDBACK:

■ **Gives us more information for decision making**

■ **Gives us better information for decision making**

■ **Checks information or instructions have been understood or actioned**

■ **Allows staff to solve problems restricting their performance**

■ **Allows management learning**

■ **May increase employee satisfaction, motivation and performance**

If you have to plan or organize anything, two-way communication is vital to making sure that it gets done correctly and in the best way possible. If you are to run a successful team, it is vital that your team gives you feedback. You need to be kept informed about how the task is going, how things could be made to work better and how you are performing. Encouraging two way communication is really a case of building up trust. If your team trusts you, they will communicate openly and often, which will enable you to do your job more effectively. "What are your views on this?" can be one of the most

effective ways of encouraging excellent ideas and will also improve the motivation of the person whose opinion you canvass. Many of us have found ourselves in the situation of having information or ideas that would help our team or organization or that we simply wanted to express – but some barrier prevented us sharing our ideas. These barriers must be removed for communication to work. Most are under your control, especially if you are a team leader. Roughly half your time should be spent listening. To get maximum value each time someone offers feedback use active listening and open questions.

MAJOR BARRIERS AGAINST FEEDBACK

■ **The boss didn't want feedback or was unapproachable**

■ **The boss never seems to listen to anything that is said**

■ **No-one asks for feedback**

■ **The staff felt that they were too junior or inexperienced or that their ideas would not be taken seriously**

■ **There was no opportunity to give the feedback**

■ **Fear of disagreeing with the boss**

If nothing is done to break down these barriers, the team will waste time and resources and become demotivated.

ACTIVE LISTENING

■ Find somewhere to talk where you will not be interrupted

■ Show interest in the person who wishes to talk

■ Listen until they have finished. The last few words are often the most important

■ Pay attention physically – nod, smile, maintain eye contact

■ Show support both in your response and actions

■ Check back to ensure you have established exactly what the sender meant to say

■ Help the sender to structure their ideas if necessary

■ Summarize and agree main points before moving on

■ Build on the sender's argument to help them. Don't substitute your own ideas

■ Try to understand their position

■ Pay attention to what they are NOT saying – this can be important as well

■ Don't let your personal views interfere with the listening

■ Relax – you listen better when relaxed

To improve the amount and quality of feedback that you receive, ask for feedback, listen to it, act upon it if appropriate and then let the person who provided you with information or an idea know what is being done about it.

■ Actively encourage feedback by asking for it

■ Use active listening skills

■ Act on feedback – do something about it – give feedback on it

■ Tell them what is happening about their feedback

■ Hold regular two-way briefing sessions

■ Build a team culture that encourages two-way communication

It is the team leader's responsibility to make sure that he or she receives enough good quality feedback. When people are asked the main reason for them not telling their boss what was going wrong or what they thought could be improved, most reply that their boss did not seem interested in their input. This is unforgivable and probably ruins any chance of getting the team to work well. Alternatively, they say that no-one asked for their opinion.

Giving Feedback To Others

Those working for you need feedback on a day-to-day basis as well as at their formal appraisals. One of the major criticisms of team leaders is often that they do not tell the people working for them where they stand. Saving up all of your information for the appraisal tries to address too many issues at once, making them harder to manage. Regular feedback on a day-to-day basis lets people know where they stand and allows them to develop and improve their skills as well as allowing any improvement to begin at once. Giving effective feedback is a critical part of task supervision and evaluation. It is also a major contributory factor in producing good team and individual motivation.

However, approaching feedback in the wrong way can demotivate the individual concerned. Everyone is sensitive to the discussion of personal performance.

Giving praise Some managers praise too little, some praise too often. The balance also varies according to who is being praised. Some individuals would not wish to be praised publicly, some would find just a word of thanks enough whilst others would prefer time off. Try to get to know what motivates individuals in your team. A good motivator uses praise only when it has been earned. Praising just to create a pleasant atmosphere is a waste of time and makes people think they are doing well when they are not.

THE FOLLOWING GUIDELINES WILL HELP YOU TO GET IT RIGHT

■ Pick an appropriate time and place
■ Be specific – both positive and negative feedback are more valuable when specific examples are given
■ Give feedback in a logical sequence
  – Measurable performance and facts
  – What this says about the individual
  – Consequences for the team or organization
  – Any resulting actions that may follow
■ Check that the person you are speaking to understands what you have said – ask questions and listen to the replies
■ Give the other person an opportunity to contribute
■ Try to take a positive approach. Even negative feedback should be aimed at helping the individual to improve their performance. For example, suggest how things can get better and give examples of recent improvements. Constructive criticism not censure is required

WHEN GIVING PRAISE TRY TO STRESS THE FOLLOWING:

- What was good about what the person or team did
- Why was it good
- What it says about them
- The impact on the team or organization

Remember that rewards are more effective if people know in advance how they will benefit for good performance. Expectations and targets should be agreed by all the parties.

You should also make sure that the targets are within the abilities of the individuals concerned. They may be tempted to agree to do too much if you ask them, so make sure that this does not happen. If you set targets too high they will never achieve them and as a result will become demotivated. The target should be realistic and challenging to allow the individual or team a good chance of success and praise, but difficult enough to develop and challenge them.

Giving negative feedback

Before you even consider giving negative feedback you must make sure that it is deserved. In all too many cases people are given negative feedback that they really don't deserve. In the majority of cases the reasons why an individual does not perform as well as required boil down to one of the following

- Not being told clearly what to do and understanding not being checked.
- Being given a task outside their capabilities.
- Not being given sufficient resources to do the job. This includes time.

All of these problems are the fault of the person delegating the job, not the person doing it. It may be a genuine misunderstanding – perhaps you thought that they had the skills required, but did you check? There is nothing more likely to sour relationships with your team than accusing them of under performing when most of the fault lies with you as a manager. If you are sure that the problem lies with someone else, then give your message carefully.

Of all areas of communication perhaps the most difficult is giving negative feedback. If the receiver becomes defensive he or she can block out most or all of your message. It is important that the message is structured and delivered so that this does not happen. The basic structure conforms to the pattern set out before, but it has been fine tuned to help you deliver the message in a way that should improve your chance of being received and understood as you intend.

Giving Feedback To Others

...Think about what you are going to write, to whom you are writing and the order in which it is to be written...

- Background – explain the general area you want to talk about.
- Explain why what you are about to say is important.
- Try to find an example of positive behaviour to set a positive tone.
- Be specific and use examples.
- Describe what happened first, don't judge. For example, "You didn't make the deadline and as a result we upset the client."
- Concentrate on specific things that can be improved or changed.
- Agree future action to prevent a repeat of the problems.
- Make sure that your message has been understood by asking open questions.

Involve the other person

Facts and events should be stressed, rather than the characteristics of the person. When you start to address the specific problems if possible try to get the individual concerned to identify the problem themselves rather than telling them about their problems; they may realize that things have not gone well and know why. In most cases people do have a reasonable idea about what went wrong. To help them to identify the problems you can use open questions and active listening. For example, "How do you think the project you did went last week? What were the areas you found caused you problems?" This approach allows them to talk through what happened. Further questions can point them in the right direction. For example, " You seemed to take a lot of time on the report, what were the problems you had?" You can also add in a further positive comment such as "Well you seemed to have problems writing a report. What were they and how can I help you to overcome them?"

In other cases the person concerned is genuinely unaware that there has been a problem. This situation requires even more delicate handling. If at all possible, try to introduce a negative with a positive. "I would like to talk about how I can help you to improve your report writing because there are a few mistakes in the one that you recently submitted."

The annual appraisal

Because the communication of information about their own performance is so important to people and has such a great impact on their motivation and development, you also need to think about how you handle this. The way that a message is delivered is critical to its understanding and acceptance. This applies just as much to the appraisal as any other situation.

Your organization may already have an appraisal process that you have to complete, but you should not just "go through the motions".

An appraisal is an opportunity to help the person to improve. Preparation is crucial. Make notes about the points that you want to get across. If the appraisal is expected to take an hour, spend at least 20 minutes reading the relevant notes, deciding what you want to say and thinking through the points to be discussed. Think about possible solutions to any problems.

When the person who is being appraised arrives, help them to relax. Many people find the annual appraisal unnerving. You will not achieve much if the other person is speechless with nerves. Explain what is going to happen, how their performance is being assessed and how any measures of performance are worked out. Stress that you are appraising to provide help and support, not to call them to account.

Then move onto more general issues, but still keep the focus on facts rather than opinions. Follow the basic guidelines for giving feedback. In each area that needs improvement agree a plan of how to achieve the aim. Also set deadlines by which targets will be met. It is essential that this is agreed between both parties.

At the end always give the other person the chance to raise any issues and to ask you any questions. Get some feedback about what they thought of the appraisal and how you conducted it. Did it help with identifying strengths and weaknesses? Did you do most of the talking? Did you use open questions?

It may be worth considering introducing "interim" appraisals, perhaps midway between the annual appraisals. Your team will find it helpful and it shows that you are committed to their development and improvement.

Don't put it off

Although it may be tempting, do not put off giving negative feedback. It is all too easy to try to avoid the potential awkwardness and conflict which may arise when giving negative feedback – after all we all want to be liked – but the person concerned needs to know that they are not performing well. On many occasions the individual or team doesn't realize that they are getting things wrong. You are helping them to improve, which in the end they will appreciate.

Communicating By Telephone

Remember that people get tired of wasting their time on unproductive telephone calls. If you can make every call productive you will become one of the most effective people in your organization.

Even if you do not use the telephone to directly generate business, it is essential to be able to use it effectively. It is vital that calls from outside the organization are handled well. To the caller *you* are the organization. How you handle the call gives an image of the whole company.

Calls from within your organization matter as much as those from people outside. It gives an image of your department, your team and you.

On the telephone the non-verbal signals used to help get a message across in face-to-face communication, such as facial expressions, are not present. All of the signals are in the voice and the conversation.

Answer the call within 4 rings and with a smile! This confirms that you are efficient and the smile will ensure that you sound positive when you answer. You may not feel like smiling, but the face muscles you use in a smile affect the tone of your voice – making it sound more positive.

The verbal handshake Introduce yourself and, if you are the one making the call, establish whether it is a convenient time to talk. This is particularly important if you are calling a mobile phone. The person taking the call may be in an inconvenient place. If the call is to a hands free car phone, for example, other people may be listening.

HAS THE CALL BEEN SUCCESSFUL?
Think about what annoys you when you try to contact people by telephone. There are some general things that tend to have an influence on the impression that a caller is left with:
- Whether the call is answered at all
- How long it takes to answer the call
- How many people have to be gone through before it is possible to speak to the right one
- Whether the person taking the call listens to what the caller has to say
- How polite the response is
- Whether the call is answered with courtesy and efficiency
- Whether the call is productive
- If both parties agree on the outcome and action
- Pressing lots of buttons and listening to automated voices and eventually still not speaking to a human being
- Talking to someone for a long time before finding out that they are not the right person to help
- Not being given the opportunity to explain what it is that you really want

Taking ownership If you take responsibility for the call, the person calling will be more relaxed. This means either that you agree to take action on their behalf or that you will see that the person who is responsible will do so, or transfer them to that person at once. Accept that you represent your organization, department or team and ensure that the agreed outcome actually happens. How many times have you been infuriated to hear, "I'm sorry that's not my area" or "I'm afraid I haven't the authority to deal with this".

Keep the call on track Make the caller feel involved. Use the caller's name, ask open questions (those which begin with what, where, how, which, when and who) to encourage them. Make appropriate noises to confirm that you are still paying attention – "yes" and "I understand". These replace the visual signals that you use when communicating face-to-face. This is particularly important if the person calling is making a complaint or explaining a problem.

Record and repeat Write down what the caller is saying and check with them that you have got it right. This confirms to the caller that you have understood what they have said. If the conversation is likely to be either long or complex, write

PUTTING CALLS ON HOLD
Before you put a caller on hold or transfer a call, let the caller know what is going to happen. Give the name and number of the person to whom you are transferring them in case the call gets cut off. Make sure that the caller understands why the transfer is necessary. For example, say "I am going to transfer you to Jim Benton, the product manager on extension 334 because he deals with the type of information that you need. There may be a moment or two of silence as the call goes through".

down the main points in bullet form during the call. This will then allow you to repeat and will give you a record of the main points for reference after the call is finished. Use the principles of active listening to make sure that you find out what the caller really wants.

Closing the call This stage is essentially an opportunity to provide the caller with any extra information that they may need and to agree any action that will be taken and by when. Make sure that the caller has your name and extension number so that they can get back to you if they need to and make sure that you take their contact number. If you agree to do something during the call, write it down as soon as the call has finished. How many times have you forgotten something that was agreed in a telephone call? If you need to, send the caller written confirmation of what has been agreed.

Using The Written Word

Though written communication has its advantages don't forget that written words are not as personal as spoken words. They don't allow an immediate response, don't allow the receiver to ask questions at the time and often take more time to digest. Verbal communications can be forgotten, but don't forget that written communications can be lost – they are not guaranteed to get through – a verbal check of receipt is always a sensible precaution.

The same basic principles that apply to verbal communication also apply to written communication. You need to decide the message you want to get across, find the best means to deliver it and make the delivery. It is as important with written messages as with verbal ones to confirm that they have been understood.

A written message gives you a permanent record. This "hard copy" can be useful. It can be referred to at any time and sent to any number of people. Written communication can allow you to put across complex ideas and information in a format that allows the receiver to assimilate it at their own pace and in their own way.

If the message you are trying to get across is personal or complex then maybe doing it in person would be better even if you then send written confirmation of what was agreed.

If you feel awkward talking to people, try to do it more often using the formats in this book to help you get it right and build your confidence. By avoiding speaking to people directly and relying instead on written communication you will isolate yourself and may lose touch with the team because people will not communicate with you effectively. So if you do not get their feedback, this may cause problems in the future.

The main forms of written communication you will probably be using at work are letters, memos (including e-mail), and reports. Most of us have to reply regularly to letters or send them out. Even if you don't, you certainly will have to send and reply to letters in your personal life – this section should help you in both areas.

STAY IN TOUCH
Do not use e-mail or memos as a way of avoiding face-to-face communication. Avoiding talking to people can lead to problems in the future.

Letters

Any letter you send (this includes e-mail) must follow the general rules of effective communication. Be simple, clear and concise and follow the logical structure of all communications.

Before you begin make sure that you are clear about the objective of your letter. Ask yourself, "What do I want to achieve with this letter?" Aim to get the message across in a way that ensures that the person receiving it will understand it. Keep the language simple. Use plain English with no jargon. Keep the letter as simple and to the point as possible. Try not to leave the reader in any doubt as to what you want the outcome to be.

It may help to imagine what you would say if you spoke to the person concerned before you start to put it on paper. This seems obvious, but many people have difficulty in putting on paper what they would have no trouble saying face-to-face.

Plan the letter before you begin to write it. Write the headings suggested by Kipling's poem *Six Honest Serving Men* (page 36) on a rough piece of paper and write out a draft.

What do I want to achieve? This is the purpose of the letter. What do you want to say to the person who will be getting the letter? If you want them to do something, what exactly is it?

Why do I need this to happen? What is the reason for writing the letter? What caused you to want to achieve the objective? Possibly give the background to the problem or question.

When? Are there any time limits? Next week, month or year? When do you want it done by?

How? Do you want to achieve your objective in a particular way, or will you leave it up to the receiver?

Where? Are there geographical or physical factors? Where do you want the meeting? Where should the delivery go to?

Who am I going to say it to? In most cases you know who the letter is going to but occasionally you may not know the name. If possible try to find out their name – "dear sir" will work, but using a name will at once encourage a positive response. If you have made the effort to use the name of the person you are writing to this will make the contents more personal. Do you need to copy the letter to other people?

...It's a good idea to write a one-page summary to put right at the front of the report...

Using The Written Word

FINE TUNE THE MESSAGE

Having clarified your message fine tune it before you put it in letter form to make sure that the reader understands exactly what you want. The mnemonic SCRAP will help:

Situation
Consequences
Resolution
Action
Politeness

Situation Sum up what the letter is about – outline the facts. For example, "Last week your delivery was late".

Consequences A development from the facts and a resulting problem or question. For example, "This is not the first time this has happened and as a result we could not complete the job".

Resolution Suggest a possible solution. "We understand that your delivery van was caught in traffic and that the journey time is now longer. Perhaps if the drivers left earlier to come to us this would remedy the problem?"

Action What you will do or expect the person getting the letter to do. For example, "Would you please ensure that your delivery van leaves early enough to get our delivery to us on time".

Politeness Even if you are upset with the person or organization to whom the letter is being sent, you need to remain polite and concentrate on the facts. If you use emotional language or insults, you are unlikely to get a positive response. "Would you please try to ensure that our deliveries arrive on time in future." Try to conclude with some expression of goodwill or at least be polite, even if it is only a basic "yours sincerely".

MEMOS

Memos are part of business life and can play a useful part in getting information across in a brief form. A memo can be used as a quick written confirmation of what happened in a conversation or meeting. A memo should be like a short sharp letter, not a rambling, jargon filled treatise. Use the SCRAP format, but keep it very short.

Making sure that the job gets done

On occasions, perhaps after a team meeting, you need to confirm who is to do what by when, and who they have to report to. This can become complicated. To make clear what is to happen you can use an action schedule at the end of the meeting. Set out the information in a simple table. The action schedule can be referred to for more detail in the text or meeting minutes. It will make it absolutely clear who needs to do what.

You must also ensure that all those people who have to complete some action are given or sent a copy of the schedule. It is often included in the minutes of more formal meetings, and is sent to everyone who attended. To enable those with actions to undertake to complete them in time, the minutes or schedules need to be published quickly enough to allow this to happen.

In the final analysis, the purpose of communication is to achieve something. Make sure that it is clear what has been decided and if anything has to be done, who it must be done by. This is what the action schedule is about. Without it, meetings are just "talking shops" that waste the time of all of those involved.

EXAMPLE ACTION SCHEDULE

Actions schedule for Stage 1 of marketing plan

Action:	Responsible:	By:	Confirm to:
Contact top 15 clients	DJP	14th October	Head of Mkt
Submit advert text	PGH	22nd October	Head of Mkt
Produce graphics	DB	22nd October	PGH
Approve advert	Head of Mkt/MD	31st October	–

Writing A Report

Writing a report can be a daunting prospect. But you are probably not being "lumbered with an appalling job", you are being trusted with something that is important to the organization. If you think there is a problem that needs addressing, you could offer to write a report about it.

Many people are promoted after writing a good report that solved a problem. Even if this does not happen, writing a report will at least mean that you understand the organization better.

Reports follow some of the logical structure of letters, but because they are usually longer than letters some additional rules apply. If your organization has a standard format, follow it, but make sure that you include all of the ingredients given below.

1. Give the present position Summarize the current situation. Cover the general background in order to put the report into context.

2. Outline the problems involved This is probably why the report is being written.

3. Detail the possibilities Set out the possible courses of action and evaluate them. It is important that there are a range of possibilities even if it is either do nothing preserve the status quo, or change to something else.

4. Make your proposals This is where you sell your ideas. You have to make the proposal attractive to the reader. Do not be tempted to omit this section in case it upsets someone or is wrong. As long as your report is logical and you use a methodical approach, then this should not be a problem. If what you propose will have a cost, make sure that the benefits are proven and stressed and that the projected costs are outlined.

The tips on page 72 *Negotiating and Getting Agreement* for persuading sceptics to give your ideas a try are useful in reports as well.

The proposal is the main body of the report. Keep the language simple and concise, making sure it is relevant to the problem and the points raised in the report so far. Avoid jargon and use plain English. Choose short words if possible.

Keep sentences and paragraphs short. Bear in mind that you want your report to be read. Pages and pages of solid text are intimidating and look boring. Try to help the reader in the way you lay out the pages. Use indents, wide margins and logical headings and sub-headings. Try to use graphics, such as charts and tables, if you can to help to put across complex information.

This structure covers the main body of the report. The other parts of the report may not be familiar to you, but they all play an important part.

Summary

Include a one or two paragraph summary of the whole report. It allows someone who does not have time to read the whole report to understand the present position, problem, possibilities and your proposal. It can be difficult to get all this into such a small space, but it is an essential part of any report. Write this section last.

Terms of Reference

This outlines the brief that you were given to write the report and directly links into the objective. Include information about who asked you to write the report and what limits you were given – what you consider were the "rules of engagement" for your report.

Objective

This is the reason for the report. For example, "to identify a cost-effective solution to the current ventilation equipment problem".

Bibliography and sources

Refer to any books or articles that you have used by listing them and referencing them into the report in the bibliography. Sources (discussions with other people rather than published information) should also be given. Include dates because information can go out of date.

Appendices

Extra information that supports the main body of the report – such as data, case studies, results of other reports that contribute to your proposal but are too long to go into the main text – should be provided as appendices. These tend to be the basic research findings. The contents of the appendices should be referred to at the appropriate point in the main body of the report.

Making a final check

After spell-checking read the report a couple of times with a break in between and get someone else to check it too.

To help you determine what goes into the appendices ask yourself, "Does the reader HAVE to have this information to make the decision ?" If the answer is "yes", it should be in the main body. If the answer is "no", put it in the appendices.

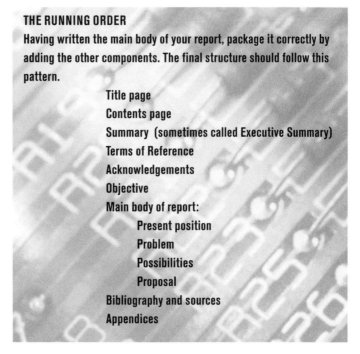

THE RUNNING ORDER
Having written the main body of your report, package it correctly by adding the other components. The final structure should follow this pattern.

        Title page
        Contents page
        Summary (sometimes called Executive Summary)
        Terms of Reference
        Acknowledgements
        Objective
        Main body of report:
            Present position
            Problem
            Possibilities
            Proposal
        Bibliography and sources
        Appendices

Negotiating And Getting Agreement

One of the most awkward communication areas is that of discussing problems that have come up and trying to get an agreement. We have already looked at giving negative feedback which is a related area. In this section we look at how to communicate effectively in those general problem situations that come up – any area where there may be conflicting views or contradictory objectives, such as negotiating resources from your boss or getting extra work from your team.

Encouraging people to consider problems they may have

The first step is to get everyone involved to agree that there is a problem to discuss at all. It is important to get people to try to identify their own problems rather than simply telling them what is wrong. This approach stops them feeling that you have identified problems that they don't think really exist, and as a consequence, ignoring your message.

By asking open questions (how, why, what) you should be able to get the other person to focus on what the problem is and enable them to find solutions. It is much better for the people concerned and your working relationship if you can help them to solve their own problems rather than just telling them what to do.

If someone has difficulty identifying problems or finding answers, try asking more questions to help them to pinpoint the problem area. For example you could ask, "How do you think that I could help you develop your skills in the technical areas?" Once they start to talk about their perceptions of the situation use active listening skills in order to help them come to an understanding of the problems and find solutions.

Play fair People view "forcing them" to give you what you want, or "conning them" as a quick fix in these situations. Neither is effective in the long term – forcing someone to do something that they do not want to will just cause a working relationship to sour and "conning" people will only work for a short time, then you will not be trusted again. Put yourself in the position of the other people involved? Would you agree to your own proposals as you have presented them? What benefit will the other people involved gain from agreement? In practical terms you have to "sell" your proposal.

TACTICS THAT MAY HELP TO PERSUADE OTHERS TO TRY OUT YOUR IDEAS OR SUGGESTIONS

■ Request a short "test" period. This does not commit them to a long term cost and will allow them further time to consider. It also gives you a chance to prove that your ideas work.

■ Confirm the overall benefits of your proposal both to the organization and to the team or individual you are trying to convince. If you can establish that there is a benefit then the chance of getting what you want are much greater. If you can, prove the benefits your proposal would bring. Make use of the following where appropriate:

Use your own figures and data to support your argument

Give examples of places where a similar approach has been successful

Provide evidence of support from other people or senior staff

Show why your proposals are an improvement

Show that it would be possible to evaluate the outcome of your idea

Show why the subject you are making a proposal about is important

Show that any costs encountered are outweighed by the benefits

Make the proposal simple to understand and clear in its reasoning

5

Identify needs
Action plan
Take action
Develop skills

Where do I need to improve?

How can I develop my skills?

Do I need support?

Developing Your Skills

To get maximum benefit from this section of the book it is important to complete all the exercises in it. They will enable you to build on the self-assessment that you have already done and plan how to improve your skills.

You will identify areas where you should improve your skills, prioritize them and make a personal development plan to help you improve. You will also consider how you could help improve the communication skills of your team members.

Watch yourself in action

The self-assessment questionnaires in chapter two will have given an indication of how good your current skills are. To improve assess your own performance from day-to-day and week-to-week.

Each time you communicate observe what you do, record how it went, and evaluate what was good and what could have been done better. This doesn't have to be a large report, just a few notes on a piece of paper about what happened and ideas for improvement. It should take about five minutes and is well worth the time. Slips of paper tend to get lost so if you have a desk diary, jot down ideas for self or team improvement in that.

Where do I need to improve ?

Draw up a self-assessment table following the example given (right). Transfer the ratings that you got in the self-assessments in chapter two. Be honest when you complete the list.

The exercise will be more accurate if you also get feedback from others – your team, peers, your boss, friends. Ask them if you communicate clearly. Do you ever miss out information or confuse them? Do you ask them if they have understood your message? Do you give your team feedback effectively whether it is praise or negative feedback? You could also try tape recording meetings, conversations, telephone calls and other verbal communication. Explain why you are doing it and ask the other people involved for their permission. Your team will probably agree because it should improve your communication skills which should help them too.

How did you do?

You will probably have identified at least three or four areas where you need to improve your skills; any less than this and either you are a brilliant communicator or perhaps you were not being as honest as you could be. The next step is to produce a specific plan to develop each skill where improvement is necessary. If time permits, try to improve the skills which you classified as "satisfactory". Why be satisfactory when you can be good?

Repeat this assessment regularly – possible annually or every six months.

Skills	Good	Satisfactory	Could Be Better
Understanding the principles of communication			
Planning a message			
Matching my message to the receiver			
Face-to-face communication with individuals			
Face-to-face communication with groups			
Giving positive feedback			
Giving negative feedback			
Using the telephone			
Briefing a team			
Running team meetings			
Letter writing			
Memo writing			
Writing reports			
Communicating with your boss			
Communicating with your peers			
Active listening and questioning others to make sure you understand them			
Talking through problems and getting agreement			

Areas Of Regular Communication

What about the communications you undertake regularly? Are you communicating effectively by using the right message and means for the situation. Do you get your message across effectively to all of those with whom you have to communicate? If not, you may be wasting time and resources. Having considered the general strengths and weaknesses in the way you communicate consider one by one the main communication events in which you engage at work.

It is important to focus development in areas of weakness that relate to the most important activities that you do at work. For example, it is unfortunate if you do not accurately express yourself when you order stationery, but if you cannot explain to your production team how you would like productivity to be improved, this is very serious.

By constructing a communication event list you will be able to consider all of the major communication areas in your working life and to analyse your performance in each. Use the example communication event list (right) to

consider how you could improve. Set out the table as shown and put in each main communication activity that you engage in together with the way you do it. For each event ask yourself the following questions: Are you using the best means of communication? Does the message get across? Do you get feedback?

To check that you have assessed it correctly why not ask the person you communicate with for their opinion?

This exercise can be particularly useful if you have to use a wide range of different communication methods. Can you identify areas where you could improve communication by adding or changing the means of delivery or the content of your messages? For example, in area three in the communication event list (right) perhaps adding an extra communication channel would improve relationships with clients and improve sales. In area four it may be a good idea to practice making the message clearer by getting feedback from the team. In example five the level of understanding with the boss could possibly be improved with the use of open and closed questions and active listening.

	Event	Who do you communicate with	Communication method	Is this the best means	Is there any feedback?	Is the message usually successful
EXAMPLE COMMUNICATION EVENT LIST						
1	Weekly sales figures	Peter Smith	Verbal 1:1	Yes	No	Tends to be rushed
2	Liaison with minor clients	Minor clients	Telephone	Yes	No	Partially
3	Sending out information to clients	Major clients	Written	Possibly	Only with verbal follow up	Partially, but needs telephone follow up
4	Giving feedback to team on performance	All team members	Verbal	Yes	Yes – but they say I am not always clear on what I want from them	Partially
5	Weekly meeting with boss	Boss	Verbal 1:1	Yes	Yes	Partially, but it needs to be clear what we want
6	Contact with other departments	Various	Verbal Telephone Written	Possibly, but I maybe don't write down as much as I should	Yes, but occasional confusion about timings and responsibilities	Partially, but we need to agree things so that both sides are clear on actions

Preparing To Write A Development Plan

Once you have identified the areas in which you wish to develop your skills, put together a plan for improvement. First use the model below to consider how you learn. You review your experiences and learn from your assessment. The next step is to plan your development. This should not be a one off event that you do only while reading this book. To really develop you need to use this circle as often as possible.

Briefly review your experiences as they happen and then every six to twelve months sit down, assess yourself and write out a formal development plan for the next period. Use the exercises in the book to help in your self-assessment and development planning regularly throughout your career.

Self-assessment will help you to discover where your weaknesses lie. A model called the *Johari Window* (opposite page) can help you think about this more clearly. It suggests that there are four areas of information about ourselves and we need to consider all of them to understand how to improve.

Information known to yourself and others
This is public knowledge. Perhaps everyone in the office knows that you are the best person to deal with a certain difficult client. Think about why you are the best at particular communication issues. What is it about your approach in those situations which helps you to communicate effectively? What do you do that is different to other people?

THE LEARNING CIRCLE

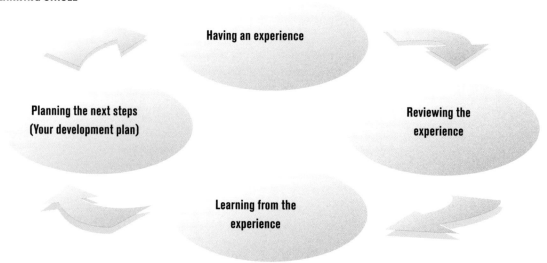

Having an experience

Planning the next steps
(Your development plan)

Reviewing the
experience

Learning from the
experience

Information not known to others What things do you alone know about yourself? For example, do you feel shy in groups but you manage to cover this up when you are at work by avoiding meetings? Are there any ways you can help yourself to overcome this problem?

Information known only to others Find out the things that others know about you, but you don't know – your own blind spot. For example, have you ever discovered from someone else that you have a habit you were unaware of – perhaps you scratch your ear or nose whilst you talk. Watching yourself on video can highlight such habits – such as saying "er" at the start of each sentence.

Discovering the blind spot emphasizes the importance of getting feedback, not just from yourself and your boss, but also from your staff and peers. There may be a range of things that you do that affect the team, the individuals in it, and their performance.

Information not known This type of information is the information that no one knows as yet. It can only be revealed through some kind of self-analysis or discovery, which may sound a little psychological and intimidating. It need not be. For example, in your life have you ever discovered that you are good at something you would never even have thought of? Perhaps you took up a hobby through your children and discovered a real talent, or you have found that you enjoy working on computers though you were trained late in your career. These discoveries fall into this category.

You probably already have ideas about how you work with people, what you do well and what not so well. Is there a pattern behind this? What jobs do you not enjoy? Why do you dislike them? What can you do to solve the problem? If you feel intimidated by some people, who are they and why do you feel that way? How can you solve the problem? Thinking carefully about these issues will probably reveal information about yourself which was previously part of the "unknown at present" area. By analysing your problems and trying to find the causes, you will find the answer and be able to tackle them.

	JOHARI WINDOW	
Known to You	Public Knowledge	Secret Knowledge
Not Known to You	Own Blind Spot	Unknown at Present
	Known to Other People	Not Known to Other People

Identifying Development Needs

By now you have identified how good you are in each of the communication areas and in those regular communication activities you undertake. Now you can use all that information to write down the things you need to do to improve your effectiveness in the problem areas.

For example, if you have identified that you have a problem with putting together your message in all communications then you might write in the space "need to use format from book to make sure my message is clear". If you keep forgetting to ask for feedback after one-to-one communications write in the space, "forget to ask for feedback – need to remember and to practice listening and use of open questions".

The chart gives an idea of the steps to take to improve your skills. Expand it to give a detailed development action plan.

Area of communication	Things you need to do to improve
Understanding the principles of communication	
Putting together your message	
Face-to-face communication with individuals	
Face-to-face communication with groups	
Giving feedback	
Using the telephone	
Briefing a team	
Running team meetings	
Using voicemail/ answering machines	
Letter/ memo writing	
Writing reports	
Communicating with your boss	
Active listening and questioning of others to make sure you understand them	
Talking through problems and getting agreement	
Other Areas	

Development Action Plan

Select the areas where you need to improve and the steps you would take to achieve this and photocopy a Development Action Plan for each.

1. Write what the skill is that you need to improve. This may be "Need to take more care in communicating with inexperienced staff – tend not to give them enough detail which means they can get confused".

2. Outline the steps needed to improve this. For example, "Write out the appropriate format from book and prepare in advance for one-to-one discussions about important matters".

3. Say whether your boss or organization could help you to improve. If any of the actions you propose would be more effective with support from your boss or the company, include what they could do to help. For example, "discuss with my boss how she may have dealt with a problem similar to the ones that I regularly encounter."

4. Put in a date by when you will have achieved an improvement or will have completed the action that you have set yourself. You must set yourself a deadline and stick to it. If you don't do this, you will suddenly find years have passed, you have done nothing to improve and as a result someone else has been selected for promotion. Remember that it is up to you to develop yourself – no one else will do it, although a good boss may help.

Development Action Plan
Development need

Actions by:	
You	**Your boss**

Organizational support?

To be completed/achieved by

Immediate Action Plan

You may find that the Development Action Plan identifies improvements that may take some months to be effective. To keep you motivated, try to achieve something as quickly as possible. For example "write down main points of message before important face-to-face meetings" or "seek feedback on my performance" can be implemented straight away. It may help to draw up an Immediate Action Plan – of steps from your Development Action Plan that can be taken at once.

Aim to find at least six improvement actions to take immediately, possibly including the four already given in the example. Both you and the team will show an immediate benefit. Your team will be motivated and encouraged by your improvement.

Promoting development and flexibility

The workplace is not static and individuals and teams constantly need to develop their skills to meet the challenges of the future. These may be as a result of technological developments, changes in legislation, new systems being introduced, or other factors that demand that the team and individuals within it improve their skills. If people do not pass on their skills and knowledge effectively then they will take their expertise and know-how with them when they leave – your company will lose a valuable resource.

If you can enable the more experienced team members to communicate effectively, especially giving feedback, they will help the development of others and will supervise that development. Asking

	Steps to Take	Notes
1	Identify areas where my communication skills can be improved and produce a written development plan to achieve this.	
2	Set up meeting to discuss personal development plan to improve my communication skills with my manager. Explain the support I would like to help me achieve my objectives.	
3	Start improving my communication at once by using the formats in the book.	
4	Introduce team briefings to be every week or two weeks.	

someone to help with the development of another individual is one of the highest compliments you, as their boss, can pay them. It shows your faith in them and as a result can improve their performance greatly as well.

Giving individual support

Draw up a team development plan by writing down the name of each team member and assessing how they perform in each of the main communication areas in which they need to improve their skills. Obviously some will not be appropriate – a new recruit may not be required to write a report – but they may need to be able to answer the phone, confirm orders with suppliers and write memos. More experienced workers may have to give feedback to others, deal with other departments and you may want them to write reports or run meetings. Your deputy needs to have the same communication skills as you.

You can then see where they may need help. Discuss this with them and come to an agreement, using the development plan formats to plan the development of each individual. Helping the team members to develop will also improve motivation within the team.

Review and update the development plans at regular intervals.

DEVELOPING COMMUNICATION IN YOUR TEAM

If all of the team are helped to improve their communication, they will understand the principles and be more prepared to communicate with you in an open way. This means that you will know what is going on more accurately, find out about problems sooner and will be able to delegate tasks that involve communication that could not previously be done. Try to improve the communication skills of all your team members. Better communication between team members will bring benefits in the following areas:

- Better understanding of your communication
- More feedback
- Better and faster skills development
- More effective problem solving
- Better motivation and self confidence
- Reduced misunderstandings – saving time and resources
- Greater mutual support and co-operation
- Higher knowledge levels within team
- More flexible response

Don't delay do it today

Help Your Boss To Communicate With You

Your relationship with your boss is as important as that with your team, so spend time getting it right. Effective communication builds trust and if you trust each other in your working relationship, it will benefit both of you. Helping your boss to communicate effectively with you will make life easier for both of you. If you feel that your boss does not understand you, does not communicate effectively, does not delegate effectively and so on, stop blaming the boss and try to think about it more logically. Perhaps your boss also has a boss who does not communicate effectively. What problems

HERE ARE A FEW SUGGESTIONS ON COMMUNICATING WITH YOUR BOSS MORE EFFECTIVELY. PERHAPS YOU COULD DISCUSS HOW YOU CAN DO THE FOLLOWING:

- Make life easy for your boss to do their job. Keep them informed about what is going on – not everything but make sure that they have the information they need and stick to deadlines.

- Take a positive attitude to your boss – respond positively even if you are not convinced and talk it through.

- Prepare ground for discussions in advance so you both know what is on the agenda.

- Consider that your boss has problems too – see the whole picture, not just your own concerns.

- Don't give your boss nasty surprises, talk through problems in good time to avoid a last minute rush.

- If there is a difficult job to do even if you don't really want your team to do it, once agreement has been reached with your boss defend the decision as your own. Do not say "The boss wants you to…"

- Discuss your development plans – the boss needs to support you in these – so he or she needs to know about them.

does your boss have? Do you see the whole picture? Do you ever ask your boss about what is going on elsewhere, or use open questions and active listening to help communication between you?

You need to help your boss to help you. If he or she is worrying about what you or your team is doing, you are probably being pestered with enquiries about whether or not things are going well. If you make sure that he or she knows what is going on, you will probably be given more freedom.

Discuss how you can communicate effectively with each other. As a first step you can tell him or her about your development plan and ask for help. Do your own assessment of your boss's communication ability using the format you used to identify your strengths and weaknesses before you meet so that you know which areas to concentrate on, but be diplomatic.

MISTAKES
Everyone worries about making mistakes and being exposed to negative feedback from superiors as a result. If your communication is poor, you and your team will probably make more mistakes. If a mistake happens, ask yourself, "Was it my own communication that allowed this mistake to happen?"

Once your boss is thinking about communication discuss all of the areas with them, identify problems and find solutions for mutual benefit. What are the areas of communication where the confusion creeps in? Try to negotiate a solution which benefits both of you.

You and your boss are a team, aiming for the same goals. To achieve what you want to you need to work effectively together. If you can communicate well, you will work well together.

6

Improve culture
Team briefings
Help your boss
Further ideas

Can my skills develop further?

How can I improve team communication?

Can I help my team's skills to improve?

Improve Communications With Team Briefings

It is not an understatement to say that the communication within an organization – the degree to which people really are able to get their messages across – sets the tone for the whole organization. If you don't feel you can get your feelings across, or you feel no one listens to you, you become demotivated and will not work as hard as you could. Bad communication also leads to more mistakes and time and resources being lost or wasted.

Effective communication is the key to the culture within the organization. If it is present, the culture will be good and people will work well together. If it is not, the organization will not work well and profits will suffer.

The same applies to your team. If workmates communicate effectively with each other and with you, they will work better together. In the final analysis, even if the rest of the organization has poor communications there is no reason why your team should. Do not worry about the rest of them – at least your team will work well together and your success may well start to change the way that others work in time.

A good way to improve communication and culture is via regular, useful, team briefings.

Team Briefings

We have seen that you can improve team performance by helping all of the team members to communicate with you – expressing their ideas, feelings and views. As well as doing this on a day-to-day basis you may also find it useful to have regular team meetings. (see page 56 *Face-to-Face With A Group*). You can take this further – and gain more benefit – by using regular, structured team briefings. This does not mean just briefing the team, but the team also giving their input on important issues, or asking questions. The advice given for communicating face-to-face with a group can be used in any situation and should ensure that the message gets across – but with a more structured and regular team briefing you can cover a whole range of issues, not just one specific issue that has to be resolved. By holding regular team briefings you will keep everyone informed about how they are doing and what is going on in the organization. It also gives the team members a chance to give feedback and to resolve any areas of misunderstanding by asking questions. Use the following format to help you to get maximum benefit from the team briefings that you run.

Progress & Performance One of the most important questions for both teams and individuals is – "How are we doing ?" It may be difficult for you to provide a specific figure, but an indication of how things have gone is helpful. If you use technical words or statistics, make sure that they are understood by all – if anyone does not understand then you have failed to communicate. The team briefing may be a good forum to praise people for good performance – if it is directly related to an item under discussion.

Policy & plans In this section you can explain existing policies and future plans – occasionally we are unsure why things happened or are done in a certain way – this allows you to explain such things to the team. In addition we all like to know what is going to happen in the future, so also explain any possible future plans – even if they are not yet fully decided. It is much better to give the team the correct information than to let them make up their own or to leave them to rely on rumours.

People The briefing session can confirm promotions, moves, changes in responsibilities and roles. It also allows you to publicly praise the work of the team or an individual if you have not done so already under "progress and performance". For example, you can mention the fact that someone may have passed a professional exam. This kind of recognition can improve staff motivation and morale substantially.

Points for action This section should cover anything that needs to be done in the future. Remember to make clear what has to be done, by whom and when. It is often advisable if it has been a fairly complicated meeting that covered a range of topics, to send out a detailed action schedule to everyone who attended the meeting. Having it in writing makes sure that everyone is aware of what was agreed and what their responsibilities are. The schedule should include deadlines by which tasks should be complete.

Improve Communications With Team Briefings

Feedback This is one of the most important parts of the briefing. It allows the team to give their ideas or to ask questions. You may also find it useful to anticipate questions that may come up so that you can have answers prepared. For example, you may have discovered in the previous week that there is a specific matter worrying some of the team. Find out as much as you can before the briefing as it is probable that the subject will come up. This also allows you to deal with it in one go – saving multiple explanations and making sure that everyone knows what is going on.

There may be questions that come up that you do not know the answers to. These need to be passed on to the person who can answer them. If there is not a full team-briefing system in place you will probably have to persuade the relevant person to answer the question on your behalf to help you keep your team informed.

STRUCTURE YOUR TEAM BRIEFING IN THE FOLLOWING WAY

1 Progress and performance

2 Policy and plans

3 People

4 Points for action

5 Feedback

Open Communication And Learning

To be effective in any job we need to be able to improve our skills and to develop. Communication allows this to happen by enabling the knowledge of the more experienced or proficient to be made available to those who can benefit from it. Everyone learns by trial and error or by using knowledge that they have gained from others. Trial and error can be costly in terms of time taken to achieve a successful outcome because mistakes are made and resources wasted. By passing on knowledge these problems can be avoided.

Many organizations have found that if everyone can be encouraged to communicate their learning and ideas freely, things get done faster and there are fewer problems. In addition, people develop skills faster which allows more delegation and less "firefighting".

If you can achieve effective communication within the team, you can develop it into a "learning team". This means that everyone takes responsibility for the development of themselves and the other people. The free communication of information, advice and support within the team allows learning to take place much more quickly than normal.

Apply some simple principles to building a learning team:

■ Understand each other's strengths and weaknesses and use them to help.

■ Assess the areas where the exchange of information and learning is most needed.

■ Have a team development plan and individual development plans.

■ Use both the things you have in common (objectives, team spirit) and the things that are different (specialist skills) as strengths.

■ Draw up a map of how information can be transferred between team members.

■ Always link the team learning to business and personal goals.

■ Reward and recognize those members of staff who help other members of the team to learn.

Further self development

You may like to develop your communication skills further. You can achieve this through ongoing self-assessment, feedback from others, training courses and reading other books. And above all you must put your ideas and discoveries into practice.

This book is also an on-going aid to your development. Do not just leave it on the shelf once you have read it. Go back to it on a regular basis to assess how you have improved and where further progress can be made.

Development is not a one off event. The people who do well are those who continuously improve their skills.

General Development Suggestions

These are a few general suggestions that will help you develop your abilities, not only in communication, but in a wide range of useful skills.

Role models and mentors

Many people have found that finding a role model or mentor can help them to develop their skills very effectively. First, what is the difference between the two? A role model is someone whose behaviour you copy because they do what you think are the right things. Your role model may be a successful person whose position you aspire to. Adopting a role model can be an effective tool for self improvement, but there is always a danger of copying poor behaviour. Also, do not forget you are not a clone – adapt what your role model does to your own style. If you don't, it may be obvious that you are copying someone else, which may provoke resentment that you are "putting on an act".

In contrast, a mentor works with you to give you support when you need it and to help you find solutions to your problems. This is particularly important when you are trying to develop your interpersonal skills. This means that you can actually access and use the mental assets of a more skilled and experienced person, saving on the time they took to gain that level of knowledge.

Finding a mentor can be one of the most effective of all forms of development, especially when it is combined with self analysis and development planning.

If you are given the chance to work with a mentor who you respect and who can give you the benefit of their experience and skills to help you develop, grab the opportunity with both hands. If your organization sets up a mentoring scheme and asks for people to join, give it a go!

OTHER SUGGESTIONS

Think about your relationships with those you work with (the team, boss and peers) – are they open and positive working relationships?

The importance of taking a positive approach to problems and people cannot be underestimated.

Anticipate problems from team members, peers or bosses; ensure you tackle problems early – before they have gone too far.

Do not be afraid to seek help and guidance from trusted colleagues or a mentor if needed.

Do not rush into anything – always take a logical approach using the ideas and suggestions in this book. A cautious approach increases the chances of doing something well and reduces the chances of a disaster!

Conclusion

Getting communication right is all about people – getting your message across effectively to different people and getting different people to get their message across to you. If you take the effort to make sure that you communicate – both ways – with others as individuals, matching your approach to them, they will feel that you are respecting them as individuals and they will return that respect.

If you use the ideas in this book and put in a little effort at improving your skills you will be surprised at how quickly and well your skills develop – so do it now !

WHATEVER THE PACE AND PRESSURE OF THE MODERN WORKPLACE, ONE TIMELESS PRINCIPLE HOLDS TRUE:

Fail to honour people they fail to honour you

Lao Tzu   6th century BC

Index

Printed and bound by Chorus-France